Banish the Night

Banish the Night

Fighting Kur, Timango, and Other Devils in New Guinea

by Leonard Barnard

PACIFIC PRESS PUBLISHING ASSOCIATION

Mountain View, California   Omaha, Nebraska

Cover illustration by John Steel

Foreword

In the early thirties an amazed world discovered that the mountain fortresses of the island of New Guinea contained at least half a million stone-age people who were not supposed to exist! Lying north of Australia in the shape of a great prehistoric monster, this island, about a tenth the size of the United States of America, since that time has been the scene of a tremendous invasion by Christian missionaries.

Missionary pilot Len Barnard recalls some of the thrilling adventures of his work among these primitive peoples in "the land that time forgot."

I have known Len and Mavis Barnard for many years. I have stayed in their home and have enjoyed their hospitality. I have been on the trail with them and have noted their indomitable faith and courage. I know of nothing more exciting than to sit around the fire at night in the Barnard New Guinea home, away from all twentieth century sounds, and, in the light of a kerosene lamp, listen to Len's missionary exploits. How often I have wished that Len would write it all down in a book. And now he has. While I regret his terrible accident, nevertheless I am glad that during his convalescence he was able to write.

L. C. Naden, President,
Australasian Division of
Seventh-day Adventists.

Contents

1

To Be a Missionary

While the American GI's were storming the beaches of Guadalcanal in 1942, the Australian forces were driving back the determined Japanese over the Kokoda Trail in Papua. I was in the Australian Army Medical Corps helping those who were wounded in the cruel jungle fighting.

As the tide of battle behind Port Moresby receded, I was assigned to the special ANGAU (Australia New Guinea Administrative Unit) caring for the Papuans and New Guineans. After taking an advanced course in tropical medicine, I was placed in charge of a hospital in Papua.

While working at the hospital admitting post at Hanuabada village one afternoon, I received a note from a senior army officer requesting me to examine fifty carriers who had just ended a lengthy and arduous trek.

These "cargo boys" were in lamentable condition, suffering from malnutrition and a variety of tropical diseases—a pitiful looking group indeed.

After examining most of the line and admitting nearly all for treatment, I noticed something different. The skin of the last six men was in healthier tone. And although lean from apparent privation, they were obviously happier. I plied them with questions in pidgin English.

"Which way you walkabout one time other fella man all together time?" (Have you been on the journey with the other men all the time?)

"Yes, sir."

"You fella kai kai all the same other fella man?" (Have you eaten the same food as the other men?)

They said they had eaten practically the same food.

I asked whether they were medical orderlies or had carried medicine to treat themselves.

"No got."

I was running out of questions, but my curiosity was not satisfied. Could they be Christians? I asked. They replied that they were Seventh-day Adventists. Great was our mutual joy when I told them that I also was an Adventist. We all enthusiastically shook hands. Their faces beamed with happiness; I was the first European Adventist they had seen since in the remote highlands their Australian missionaries had been forced to leave them the year before.

That evening these fine Christian men came to see me. The tropical waters of the Coral Sea were lapping lazily against the wooden stilts of the hut built over the water. As the full moon sailed silently through the coconut palms, my visitors recounted their arduous experiences of the past several months.

Early in 1942 when it had become obvious that the ambitious Japanese would overrun New Guinea, the government ordered evacuation of all foreign civilians. Among these were the veteran Adventist missionary pastors A. J. Campbell and S. H. Ganger, who had pioneered at recently explored Kainantu and Bena Bena, New Guinea. Trusted Adventist nationals from another island where the gospel had been established for several years moved in.

Only recently brought from their coastal village, these Mussau islanders were bewildered when left alone among the savages of the untamed hinterland. Tribal fighting was almost a daily occurrence. Nevertheless, resolving to be true to God regardless of the cost, these men witnessed for Him whenever opportunity made it practical. It had not been many years since they themselves had been transformed from degrading heathenism.

Shortly after the Japanese withdrew, the Australian army decided to reconnoiter a trail from Kainantu in the hinterland through unexplored country to Kerema on the coast. The bold expedition would pass through dreaded cannibal country not yet traversed by white men. An Australian army officer was placed in charge of this patrol, and he selected fifty islanders as carriers, including the six mission workers.

In the cannibal country called Fories, where their intrusion was resented, the expedition was twice ambushed and viciously attacked but was able to fight its way out. Every day became a nightmare under the persistent savage harassment. Although the guns of the guards kept the primitive warriors at bay, to avoid constant fighting the patrol had nevertheless to keep moving.

Still far from the coast, struggling on and on over the seemingly endless mountains, they eventually came to the coastal lowlands. Here amid flooded rivers and crocodile-infested swamps continually hampering their progress, their supplies ran out. For two weeks they had no regular food.

In desperation some of the party ate leaves of different trees and became ill; the mission lads cooked theirs and did not become ill. Morning and evening they withdrew from the company to commune with their heavenly Father and implore His help.

One day pig tracks were seen. A shout of excitement roused the weary line. Darting into the bush, carriers soon hunted the animal down and returned with their trophy trussed to a pole on which it was triumphantly carried till the end of the day when it was roasted. Portions were passed round, and the treat was ravenously devoured by all except the mission group. In vain the army officer tried to persuade them to eat. They refused. They felt to do so would compromise their convictions against eating unclean flesh.

Conditions became more grim. Dense, tangled jungle thwarted the progress of the patrol, and they had to hack their way forward. As the men grew weaker every day, sickness loomed ever present. One man became too weak to walk, and, although most of the others were too weak to assist, the mission men offered to carry their comrade until he regained strength. At times they were so feeble that they would stop hourly and pray.

Emerging at last from the jungle, the company with great relief saw the upper reaches of the Purari River. This meant they could float downstream by canoe. And a few days later they came to a riverside village where food and help were offered them. Finally, after three interminable months of grueling hardship and constant danger, the expedition reached Kerema on the steamy Papuan coast.

After their ordeal the men were shipped to Port Moresby, then sent to our group for medical examination. The striking contrast between the mission lads and the other carriers left an indelible impression upon my mind and awoke in me a desire to be a missionary.

2

"Me Fella Ready Along Die Now"

As the war closed, I was stationed at Madang on the northern coast of New Guinea as officer in charge of the hospital there. A few days after arriving, I was visited by an impressive young man of Mussau named Mamatau. He said he was a Seventh-day Adventist and wanted to talk with me. Unable to break away from my medical tasks, I invited him and two other Adventist young men on the hospital staff to visit me that night.

As this was the beginning of the Sabbath, Mamatau, Etie, Sam, and I worshiped our heavenly Father together. I was the first European Adventist they had seen since prewar days. Mamatau, the leader, told me their story.

While passing through Madang on a trip to the highlands, Pastor Gander had left these Mussaus in a village nearby, in response to a call for an evangelist. They did not apostatize after the Japanese invaded the country but raised up a church in the jungle by their faithful witness, one of their number, Masikuku, dying from disease at his post during this period. Despite their hardships, this night their hearts were full of happiness for what God had done for them during the years of occupation.

Following the Japanese landing at Madang the New Guineans with whom the Adventist workers were staying left their coastal village to build on a ridge a few miles inland. The Mussaus went with them and soon erected a church and a school. A few months later they were surprised when summoned to Madang by the Japanese commandant.

Fearfully they answered the summons. The Japanese captain

(5)

eyed the group suspiciously and informed them that they had been reported as teaching English in school as well as speaking it in church. He recited further accusations of messages sent to the Australians about the movement and strength of the Japanese forces and demanded to know whether these things were so. Mamatau replied that they did teach and preach in simple English but had not sent the messages.

The officer curtly ordered them to cease using the English language—as the Australians would not be returning—and decreed woe to anyone rash enough to send messages to them. Mamatau respectfully answered that they taught English so that the New Guineans could read the English Bible for themselves as well as during church services. But the captain repeated his command and dismissed the men.

Several weeks later they were again summoned before the captain. This time the angry officer demanded why they had defied him by continuing to speak English in their school and church. He charged them not to preach Christianity, citing a new order allowing only the emperor of Japan to be worshiped.

To this Mamatau replied with deference that he could not refrain from preaching the gospel. The officer's face flushed. Drawing his sword, he warned Mamatau and his friends to comply or he would cut off their heads.

Slowly they wended their way home. To obey meant surrendering their faith, but to refuse meant death. There was no missionary leader from whom to seek advice, but they could pray to the Master Missionary. So, stepping into the jungle, they besought God with deep anguish for His divine guidance. They loved to teach His gospel, but if they were killed, who would help the congregations?

The Lord's instructions were clear: Go, teach, and preach. Had He not said He would be with them to the end? So their united decision was that they would continue.

Two Sabbaths later an enchanting tropical morning dawned. Under the clear blue sky a cooling breeze blew from the coast, scented with the exotic perfumes of flowering shrubs and trees. Brilliant butterflies fluttered leisurely by. All nature seemed to join in an anthem of praise to its Creator. Eating early, then washing and dressing beside the refreshing stream, the village folk strolled up to the thatched church on the hill. With a tattered and torn picture roll the Sabbath School was held, followed by a simple church service conducted by the leader.

Suddenly a detachment of gesticulating and yelling Japanese soldiers swiftly surrounded the church. Shouting as he approached, a soldier seized Mamatau by the arm and attempted to drag him outside. Cried Mamatau: "You fella banishim finish house lotu, me fella no can run away. Please allow in me finishim lotu." (You have surrounded the church so we cannot run away, so please allow me to finish the meeting.)

Reluctantly the soldier released his grip, standing outside the entrance with bayonet fixed.

Mamatau pleaded for the congregation to be faithful to God even at the price of life itself. He and his friends, who had come to teach them about the great God above, were ready to die. Kneeling in prayer, Mamatau in a choked voice commended his flock to the divine Shepherd. They sang a farewell hymn. Then, believing it would be their last opportunity, the heroic missionaries shook hands with each member of the congregation.

When the last one had made his exit, the three evangelists purposefully walked over to the Japanese captain. "Did I not tell you," the officer demanded, "that I would behead you with this sword if you refused to obey my orders?"

"Tasol, me fella ready along die now." (Yes, sir, and we are ready to die now.)

This courage startled the officer, whose heart had already been touched by the tearful partings. Just as he was willing to die for his emperor, these men were willing to die for their God.

He conferred with his soldiers, then announced that because he was impressed by their fidelity he would allow these men to worship their God as they wished as long as they did not send messages to the Australians. Relieved beyond expression, the three willingly agreed.

When he had finished, Mamatau smiled and said, "Me fella all the same Shadrach, Meshach, and Abednego."

3

A Stupid Mistake

After my guests had departed I went to bed, but not to sleep. I kept thinking about my future. The war was about over. What should I do when discharged? Could I become a missionary? "O God," I prayed, "if this be Thy will, open the way for me." This became my all-consuming ambition.

When the war ended, I applied to the mission board in Sydney. The reply was deeply disappointing. Because the mission was in the process of reorganizing its disrupted work, no vacancy existed.

My faith sagged. I did not then realize that the Lord was still leading and that I was not yet prepared for the work He was planning to give me.

After my discharge I joined the struggling public health department of Papua-New Guinea and was sent to administer the hospital at Bogia, ninety miles along the coast from Madang. There I learned to treat leprosy.

Before the close of my two-year term of government service the mission invited me to treat lepers in the highlands in a joint government-mission hospital. Thus happily joining the mission staff in 1948, I at last realized my ambition.

On a bleak day in June, 1949, my wife and three-year-old daughter Sharyn and I flew into Mount Hagen in a Dragon biplane. The ancient plane battled the elements valiantly and brought us inland to Togoba, eight miles westward in the captivating Nebilyer Valley, flanked on the west by a perpendicular escarpment always charming in its ever-changing moods.

Greeting us cheerily as we alighted from the plane, the local government officer lurched and bounced us a mile to the end of the primitive road in a battered army jeep. Then we plodded for seven miles the muddy, mountainous trail suitable only for pigs to travel. A burly New Guinean named Wagie carried Sharyn on his broad shoulders while the rest of us puffed uphill and slipped and slid down the filthy trail for three interminable hours in the unaccustomed 7,000-foot altitude.

Mud-splattered and weary, we scaled the last ridge to stand on the location of the future 500-patient colony—600 acres covered with tall swamp reeds called *pit pit.* Home was a hut of *kunai* grass, with plaited bamboo for floor and ceiling. Full of enthusiasm, I visualized lines of neat buildings on the property, surrounded by acres of garden, with hundreds of lepers successfully treated. But for my young wife with our small daughter the dismal situation produced only tears.

Although there is still much to learn about leprosy, the oldest known disease, progress has been made, and modern drugs do give a measure of hope to the formerly hopeless.

For centuries the people of this large and populous area had been slaves to an evil spirit called Kur. Driven by fear, they bowed down and worshiped sacred stones dedicated to him. We were there to introduce Christ in place of the stones, and freedom in place of fear.

After six weeks the president of our Coral Sea Union Mission, Pastor H. White, visited us, together with four other senior missionaries, Pastors C. Hart, E. A. Boehm, C. Pascoe, and H. W. Nolan, who were surveying highlands for mission development.

That evening, a cold, wet night, with water dripping from the grass roof all around the house, the first Togoba Hansenide (leper) Colony board meeting was held. We seemed to be a frigid island in a sea of water, mud, and high mountains. But we brightened the situation with a fire in the living room on a sheet of flat iron covered with soil, a common practice, and sat around the blaze until eleven o'clock in the cheery atmosphere formulating plans. Before retiring, as a safety precaution, I poured water over the glowing embers.

2—B.T.N.

Chiming peals of the midnight hour on my wife's treasured engagement clock were the last sounds I heard before drifting into slumber. At the next sound—dripping water? or crackling fire? I reluctantly opened my eyes.

Fire indeed! An ominous red glow silhouetting the bedroom doorway! Springing out of bed, I wakened my wife, rushed into the living room, shouted to the visitors. Surfacing from a deep sleep, one of them dashed into the room yelling, "Where are they? Where are they?" He thought we were being attacked by hostile New Guineans.

But the reply was blazing at the end of the room. Eager flames spread along the ceiling hungrily devouring the walls, greedily sucking air through the burnt hole in the ceiling, and carrying flames to the tinder-dry grass roofing above. Frantically I beat at the flames with a bag. All we owned was contained in this house. Was it all to be destroyed?

Hastily seizing bundles of their goods, all our guests but one rushed outside. But Pastor Hart was too dazed to understand the reason for the confusion, but finally aroused, and he hastily exited.

Presuming my wife would have taken little Sharyn outside after I had awakened her, flames all around me, and realizing the futility, I grabbed the radio near the door and dashed outside to hear the startled men shout, "Your wife is still inside!"

"Oh, God help me!" I prayed. How could my dear wife and daughter be alive in such an inferno? Rushing inside, I saw my wife, shocked into inaction, dreamily putting on her dressing gown in the swirling flames and smoke.

I snatched Sharyn, screaming with terror and still clutching her favorite doll, from her cot. The doorways were smothered in flames. We were trapped. Above our bed was a small opening used as a window. Maybe we could squeeze through it.

Climbing onto the bed, I helped my dazed wife scramble through the opening, then dropped Sharyn to her. Heaving and shoving, I finally forced my way through.

Emerging from the pall of smoke, we all gazed back at the spot where our house had stood, now one huge ball of smoke and leaping flames. Ninety seconds had separated us from a horrible death. We thanked our heavenly Father for sparing us.

The apparent cause of the fire was hot ash that had been carried into the ceiling when I poured water onto the burning embers. This ash had smoldered until it burst into flame.

Bedraggled, we moved out of Togoba early in the morning. Losses included valuable office records, and movie film just taken on the trip through the highlands. The few articles of clothing were shared among us, the comic effect drawing laughs from our otherwise sad hearts.

Still suffering from shock, my wife was carried on a crude stretcher made by eager, crowding, sympathetic highlanders.

To them our disaster was no surprise. Had not our house been built on a ceremonial ground dedicated to Kur? They intimated that we had desecrated the sacred ground and provoked his wrath.

That day we flew to the coast, where the mission and many gracious friends helped rehabilitate us. Arriving back a few weeks later, we were joined by F. L. Aveling and his family. He had a commission to set up a sawmill, cut timber, and build. And by struggling against almost insurmountable odds, he eventually made a notable contribution to the colony.

Before permanent buildings could be erected, however, we built temporary huts for staff and patients, as I was anxious to commence treatment for the thousands of hansenides (lepers) scattered throughout the highlands. Nine months after our initial trip into Togoba our first patients were admitted.

In June, 1950, Misses Olive and Elsie Pearce arrived from New Zealand, our first nurses. At this early stage the hospital was operated under very discouraging conditions; yet these two, forerunners of a noble band of nurses, treated lepers with medical practices of a high caliber, given unstintingly.

As news of our activities spread throughout the valleys and over the mountains, the number of patients steadily increased to several hundred. We felt we were at last making inroads into this serious disease in the highlands of New Guinea, helping to outflank the enemy of body and soul.

4

The False God Kur

Each Togoba clan chief has his own sacred stone symbolizing Kur, the spirit they worship. Usually small enough to fit in the palm of a large hand, the round stones are called female and the long ones male. Rarely carved, they are always secured from a distant land. When about to fight their *biduas* (enemies) or when serious illness strikes, they pray to these stones and offer them pigs' blood.

For more elaborate ceremonies, the annual sing-sings, the sacred stones are decorated with red ocher. Always on an eminence facing eastward, the ceremonial ground is a rectangular area bordered on three sides with sacred casuarina trees. The eastern end is open. Down the center of the courtyard are circular mounds of earth, about three feet high and two feet in diameter, bound with hewn planks, a sacred tree growing in each. Under these trees pig fat is buried. About twenty feet apart, the mounds could easily be taken for altars. Here the devil worshipers conduct rites that still mystify the white man.

At the western end of the open courtyard is a hut where the Togobas deposit such valuables as bird-of-paradise plumes, large pearl shells called *kinas,* spears, and bows and arrows, all of which are used as decorations in the sing-sings. Behind this treasury hut is an enclosure bordered by a twelve-foot-high fence where in long huts the sacred stones are kept and the mystical homage to Kur is offered. Women are rigorously prevented from entering. If one does enter, she may be punished by death.

For the first two days of the sing-sing, the priests of Kur

chant mysterious incantations to the sacred stones. Finally an oblation of pigs' blood is poured over the stones. During the ceremonies large amounts of the best cooked food are offered to Kur, then eaten by the men. That night the men sleep on the dirt floors of the long, low huts, their almost naked bodies tightly packed together. Fires lighted every few feet keep them warm.

The third day the men smear their bodies with a foul-smelling oil from a rare jungle tree, bedeck their heads with brilliant displays of bird-of-paradise plumes glistening in their iridescent glory, and paint weird designs on their faces with colored powder. Then, completing their grotesque masquerade by arming themselves with bows and arrows, spears, or tomahawks, the men emerge from the sacred enclosure for the climax of the three-day ceremonial, the sing-sing itself.

The ground reverberates as hundreds of feet stamp with the rhythmic beat of jungle drums. Circling round and round the sacred trees in the courtyard, they sing veneration to Kur and departed men of valor in dirge-like monotones. The whole effect of gaudy display and monotonous sound appears to hypnotize the primitive mind. It produced a powerful, depressing effect on me.

These special sing-sings were the very hub of religious life. More common were the *muga* sing-sings, also important social gatherings which culminated in a feast, when pigs and *kinas* were exchanged. These transactions once formed the backbone of the economic system, when debts were liquidated and deals were settled publicly. It was common to see hundreds of pigs tethered and hundreds of *kinas*, decorated with gum and ocher, waiting on the grass for exchange.

I have often wondered if I could not see in this elaborate heathen ritualism perversions of Old Testament worship forms. In the days of ancient Israel heathen worship was often conducted in groves. God complained that Israel "set . . . up images and groves in every high hill, and under every green tree." 2 Kings 17:10.

While treating, housing, and feeding the hansenide patients, we decided to erect a church. We considered several sites, but none equaled the place where our house had stood before the fire. Our second house had been built nearer the office, so we decided to build the church on the old sing-sing ground. While some of the local Togobas indulged in doubtful headshakings, a nearby chief agreed to construct the house of worship by contract.

I assisted by leveling the sloping ground with our newly acquired tractor and cultivator. Out of the cheering mob that had gathered while I was driving to the site, an exuberant young fellow jumped onto the front axle. Before I could stop, he was bounced off, a rear wheel rolling over his body and a tine of the cultivator deeply gashing his muscular buttocks.

Immediately the cheering changed to wailing. His friends crowded around the young man, watching the blood streaming from his ugly wound. I rushed him up to our clinic, and upon examination was relieved to discover that the tractor wheel had caused no internal injuries or bone fractures. I sutured the deep gash and placed a drain in the wound, and the patient made an uncomplicated recovery.

Nevertheless this incident cast such a gloom over the community that the work progressed sluggishly. One day I watched the workers as they attempted to raise two heavy seventeen-foot posts held together by two crossbeams near the top. They planned to push this cumbersome framework upward with two forked poles until the parts were nearly vertical and then drop them into holes. Several were shouting instructions at the same time, confusing the two pushing groups and another group pulling with a rope.

Without warning, just as the poised posts were ready to drop into the holes, one of the pushing poles slipped. With a sickening thud the heavy timbers struck the ground. It seemed that none of the workers had been struck by the falling framework, but one form farther away lay face downward. Dashing over, I saw a man struck with devilish accuracy on the top of his head by one of the forked pushing poles. His skull had been perforated.

As I bent over the bleeding victim, I realized he would not survive. A wild melee of primitives crowded around, already daubing themselves with mud and throwing dirt into the air to demonstrate their mourning. The air rang with their despairing wails.

On impulse, I swung around, in time to see wild-eyed Temba, one of the workmen, raise his ax above my head. Leaping to my feet, I quickly disarmed him, but a look of hatred lingered in his eyes.

As the body of the dead man was carried away, the lamentations grew louder and louder. Yells across the adjacent gully informed the father of the unfortunate youth of the distressing tradegy that had befallen his only son. Overcome with anguish, he severed four of his fingers with one deft stroke of his tomahawk. Blood streaming from his hand, he frantically raced across the gully to meet the frenzied mob.

In despair I wearily trudged back to my house. My wife and the two nurses, who had only recently arrived, were preparing lunch. Our six-year-old was lying on a rug on the floor as I mounted the steps and opened the door into the living room. Turning, I met the glaring eyes of Temba. With several other men armed with long fighting spears, he had followed me to the house.

Shouting, Temba sprang up the steps, accusing me of the death of the lad because I had built the church on the sing-sing ground. Assuring him of my deepest sympathy and my willingness to make any reasonable compensation, I told him also that I refused to negotiate while he and his friends were in such a threatening mood.

Temba moved to enter the house. I shut the door and fastened its flimsy latch. He pushed it open. Three times I shut the door, and three times, spurred on by his supporters, he pushed it open. Finally I warned Temba not to do this again. But he was now beyond reason and advanced once more. The situation was desperate; so, stepping up to him, I shoved him down the steps.

He walked to the side of the steps below me, thick lips curled

as if in anticipation of savage revenge. Looking up, he uttered
not a word, though intense hatred burned in his bloodshot eyes.
The spell was broken. Noticing his helplessness, his friends reluctantly followed him as he slunk away to catch up with the
mourners still trailing across the gully. All through the encounter silent prayers had been ascending from all of us in the house.
I am sure guardian angels protected us.

After this I engaged another group of men to complete the
church. The new supervisor was Yobik, a Christian, who cau-
tioned his laborers to work expeditiously, their hearts continually uplifted to God, who would enable them to finish their
task to His glory. Each morning, before a hammer was lifted,
the God-fearing Yobik led his laborers in prayer and asked his
heavenly Father for protection.

Steadily the work advanced, and soon the framework was
ready for its *kunai* grass roofing and plaited bamboo sides.
When the last rafter was nailed to the peak of the roof, the
carpenter was about to toss his hammer thirty feet to the
ground before climbing down. He called to the men below to
beware the falling hammer; then he tossed it to one side. The
falling hammer struck one of the laborers who was absent-
mindedly walking by, splitting his forehead to the bone. Although he was severely shaken, his skull had not been fractured.
After being sutured, the wound healed quickly—a great relief to
me.

The church was completed without further misfortunes and
dedicated to the worship of the true God. For several years a
host of tribesmen joined hearts and voices in thanksgiving to
their blessed Redeemer in this chapel. Thus paeans of praise
replaced the dirges of heathenism, and the supremacy of the
true God was vindicated among the highlanders of New Guinea.

5

As months mounted into years, and confidence in modern therapy increased, more and more leprosy patients clamored for admission to the colony. Instead of the old treatment of painful injections of chaulmoogra oil, we administered DDS (diaminodiphenyl sulphone), given orally twice a week. Although this did not offer any radical cure, in most cases where treatment was begun early it did arrest the course of the disease.

Among those who came in for treatment in the early years was Kai, a filthy loincloth and a bunch of leaves his only clothing. For a while he was lost among the many other patients, but then we noticed that he attended worship regularly. Kai became deeply interested in spiritual things, making himself useful as an interpreter in the church and eventually joining the baptismal class.

Soon the colony's first baptism was held in the Turuk River. It was satisfying to see the firstfruits of our struggle against heathenism symbolically buried and resurrected with their Lord. Later the small group, Kai among them, gathered near the hospital where their many friends shook their hands. I shall never forget the sight of these converts, their faces beaming with joy under the arch of a perfectly formed rainbow produced by a nearby rainstorm.

Hearing that two local chiefs named Gip and Wai were preparing for a Kur sing-sing, Kai asked them to visit the colony. Upon their arrival he took them into the church. That week the Sabbath School lesson had discussed the giving of the law on

Mount Sinai, leaving a deep impression on Kai. Hanging from the rostrum was a picture roll depicting God, in flaming majesty, giving His law to Moses. Pointing to this graphic picture, Kai told his guests of the true God who created the world and everything in it. He explained that God expected man to obey His law, just as the government wanted all tribesmen to keep its laws.

Kai, deeply in earnest, displayed considerable persuasive power as the chiefs listened in rapt attention. When he had finished, they were convinced that they should abandon their worship of Kur, because this displeased the great God of the heaven and the earth. Though they knew they would encounter opposition from some of their tribesmen, they agreed to do this.

As the chiefs left, I told Wai that a group from the colony would visit him and his people the following Sabbath. At the appointed time we threaded through the gardens of *kau kau,* crossed two streams, and climbed a steep ridge to the tribal sing-sing ground.

As we approached, we all sang lustily, " 'E got place where 'e good fella more"—pidgin English version of "There's a land that is fairer than day." Surely the mountains in this part of New Guinea were beginning to break forth into singing.

We found Chief Wai sitting with a group of his men. The atmosphere was decidedly unfriendly, and Wai received me coolly. Obviously the tribesmen were reluctant to relinquish their sacred stones. To avoid embarrassment, I assured them that we had not come to take away their valued stones unless they wished to serve the living God. All we wanted to do was to tell them about this great God who was superior to all other gods.

At the rear of the main group of men stood three others who had smeared dirt on their bodies to show their displeasure. Behind them rose the tall barricade surrounding the sacred area that held their holy stones. They were guarding the entrance to this inner sanctum. Across the pathway I noticed several long twigs pushed into the ground. This is the New Guinea way of saying, "Keep out."

Then Kai stepped forward with the picture roll showing Mount Sinai and told the people in their own language about the "big fella Papa on top" who gave His law to men for their own good and wanted them to obey it.

Slowly they thawed, and prejudice gave way to interest. They drank deeply of the words of life and were intrigued by the story of a God who loved them so much that He wanted to take them to a better land. This God was very different from Kur, who offered no comfort for the future and had to be continually appeased. At this juncture Chief Wai stood up and, speaking for the tribe, asked if we would send them an evangelist to instruct them how to live in accordance with the wishes of the "big fella Papa" above.

As the sun dipped behind the western mountains and I was about to leave, the chief, to my utter amazement, asked us to follow him and collect the sacred stones! Somewhat diffidently I entered the enclosure. The huts inside had recently been renovated for the approaching sing-sing. Near the entrance to one of them was a little grotto in whose dark and mossy recesses were hidden the objects of devotion. Each clan leader except one stepped forward and grasped his treasured stone. Then we walked outside. One by one, with dignified ceremony, each man made a short speech and ostentatiously handed me his stone until there were fifteen. We took these back to the mission as evidence that another tribe had disowned Kur and acknowledged the superiority of the God of heaven.

A few days later we made a visit to Gip's tribe. On this occasion Pastor F. T. Maberly, recently appointed the first president of the Western Highlands Mission after successfully pioneering mission work among the tenacious warriors of the Wabag valley, accompanied us. This tribe also gave up its stones.

At the request of the people of Chief Wai's tribe, Pastor Elwyn Martin, the local district director, decided to send a national evangelist. I offered an interpreter, who accompanied him to the village about a week later.

As the two neared Wai's sing-sing ground, they were accosted by a group of unfriendly men. The missionaries explained that

they had been invited by the chief. But they were threatened
with death. One man picked up a stout stick and said he would
beat them to death if they did not move quickly. They fled.

A deluge of rain descending just then increased the dejection
of the evangelist and the interpreter. It was too late and too far
to return to the hansenide colony. A sympathetic tribesman
offered them a deserted hut in which to sleep. They were able
to build a fire, but no food was given them. The following
morning they returned to us crestfallen and hungry.

Eight days later a party of excited men came at dusk to the
colony bearing a crude stretcher on which lay a child, the bone
above her elbow protruding through her flesh. She was in acute
pain. Nine-year-old Piam had fallen off a big rock while playing.

The nurses prepared the instruments and anesthetized the
patient. While I was reducing the fracture, a sudden commotion
outside the door of the operating room heralded a rushing de-
mented man, Piam's father. Grief stricken, he had smeared his
body with mud and severed a finger with his tomahawk.

With blood dripping from the stump, he rushed in, knocking
sterilized instruments flying. Obviously believing his unconscious daughter was dying, he pushed through to the operating
table and clutched the girl to him. He poured out his sorrow in
loud sobs and unintelligible words. We were unable to pull him
away until helped by several nurses. They took him from the
room, still loudly protesting and with blood trickling from the
stump of his finger.

Thus freed, we completed our task, applied a plaster cast,
then carried little Piam to the grass hut ward. There her father,
now composed, tenderly cared for her.

While visiting the patient the following morning, I noticed a
lad looking intently at her father. He was the interpreter who
had accompanied the evangelist to Wai's village. I asked him
why he was so interested in Piam's father. He replied excitedly,
"This fella man tasol make 'im big fella trouble time me fella
visit 'im village bilong 'im." (This is the very man who made the
big trouble when we visited his village.)

From this time on, Piam and her father were faithful worshipers at the colony; and, upon returning to their village, they proclaimed the gospel to their friends. Thus the medical ministry softened a hard heart and helped further Christianity in Wai's village.

While I was sitting in my office one day, Kai entered with a worried look on his face. "Sir, me got liklik talk." (Sir, I have a few words to say.)

I listened while he pleaded for permission to return to his village with a picture roll to tell his people of God's salvation. But I knew that his village, fourteen miles distant, was situated on a small rise in the middle of a swamp and that to reach it meant two arduous hours of wading through a filthy, mosquito-infested quagmire.

I reminded Kai of his physical condition. Although the disease had been arrested, it had left his feet partly paralyzed, deformed, and ulcerated, his hands crippled and almost useless. Further, I told Kai that although he was now baptized, God would not expect him to start evangelistic work until he was much improved in health, that his first duty was to stay at the colony and continue taking treatment.

But Kai was undaunted. Looking me boldly in the eye, his voice full of conviction, he replied, "Leg belong me no good, hand belong me no good, skin belong me no good, tasol neck belong me good fella." In other words, though his hands, feet and skin were not in good condition, his voice was strong. Therefore he could tell his people of God's love while God would care for him.

I could not dampen his zeal, and the following day he was fitted with new sandals and given bandages, dressings, and medicine. Before he set out, we commended him to our compassionate Saviour, who, I feel certain, has special regard for hansenide patients. Unsteady in gait but firm in purpose, Kai said, "Time me finish 'im house lotu me like you come tambu 'im." (When I have finished building a church I want you to come and dedicate it.) He started the long trudge to his village.

Shortly after, Pastor Martin sent a man to help Kai, and a few weeks later Kai sent word that the church had been completed. He intimated that one of his toes was in bad condition, requesting that I bring instruments to amputate it. I hoped that only minor attention would be required.

On Friday Pastor Martin, Mr. Aveling, and I began walking through the filthy swamp. The water and mud sometimes reached our knees. At one place we were forced to crawl between the mud and low undergrowth. But how could we complain after the crippled Kai had gone so willingly before?

The Sabbath morning sun splashed light on the surrounding scene. The mountains, rising steeply to 13,000 feet, formed a velvety purple backdrop to the neat house of worship, decorated with a profusion of bush flowers, including exquisite orchids.

After the dedication service conducted by Pastor Martin, the eight leaders of the local clans arose while the chief told us that they were grateful for the true God, who meant much more to them than Kur, and that they therefore wanted to surrender their sacred stones. They ceremoniously brought them to the altar, where they were left, inert and impotent, a continual reminder of the tribe's repudiation of heathenism.

Following this service I examined Kai's offending toe. I learned that as he was eager to assist with the construction of the church, Kai had struggled up the nearby mountain to obtain timber. Ignoring the acute pain and the ugly appearance of his toe, he had tied vines to poles and pulled them one at a time as he slid downhill. The toe had become gangrenous; therefore it had to be removed. I told Kai that for the operation he would have to be carried to Togoba.

"Tasol who can turn 'im talk suppose me go? God enough along look out 'im me suppose me stop." (Who will act as interpreter if I leave? God is able to care for me if I stay.) I told Kai that his primary duty was to get well. But he resisted my advice so strongly I finally relented and decided to operate in the village, knowing that the God in whom he trusted so implicitly would help him.

A crude table of poles prepared, Kai was helped on top and given an injection of morphine. In this operating room the sky was the ceiling, dirt was the floor, and half-naked bodies the walls. The troublesome member of Kai's left foot was cut away, and in a few days the wound healed perfectly.

Within four months Kai and his helper raised up a church of 110 worshipers, of whom thirty-two were preparing for baptism. The local chief forbade the worship of stones in his area and ordered everything prepared for the Kur sing-sing destroyed.

Some time later the indefatigable Kai walked three hours to Kuli village, where some of his relatives lived. They had not yet heard of the true God. He gathered the people and talked to them from midmorning till dusk, imploring them to depart from the worship of cold stones that can neither speak, nor see, nor hear. After sunset the men built a large bonfire, around which they gathered, and requested the evangelist to tell them more of the wonderful story. Using the three picture rolls over and over again, Kai continued talking till dawn.

Breakfast over, Kai wearily lay down to sleep; but the chief waked him, saying he wanted to hear more. Delighted at the receptiveness of his listeners, Kai roused himself and resumed his oration. About midday the evangelist from his village arrived, and most readily Kai handed over the talking to him.

On another occasion a relative of Kai's was in childbirth for several days. Pigs were killed by the heathen relatives to placate Kur, but to no avail. Early on the fourth day it was obvious that the woman's condition was critical, so the midwife, whose lack of knowledge was matched only by her incredible filth, decided to call the witch doctor.

Upon his arrival with his ceremonial spear and charms, he stated the price of his services—one female pig and several fowls. After lengthy incantations with his charms, and loud, unintelligible cries, he thrust his spear repeatedly into the ground. When it appeared to be stuck firmly and resisted any attempt to pull it out, the witch doctor indicated that the spirit was holding it and was giving him a message.

According to the witch doctor the spirit demanded that the favorite dog of the family be killed, its blood offered to Kur, and its flesh eaten. Filled with desperate grief, the family performed the mournful task. But this remedy also proved futile, and the woman's life continued to ebb.

Late in the afternoon one of the women suggested they call Kai. Much had been heard of his new God; and although they did not believe in Him, they reasoned that there would be no harm in trying His power. It was plain that the woman would die in a few hours unless help superior to Kur's came quickly. So the request was sent.

Kai readily responded. Taking his treasured Bible, although he could not read, he waded through the intervening half mile of quagmire. Arriving at the dirty hut he dismissed the heathen midwife and mourners, and entered. Tenderly Kai urged the dying woman to believe in Jesus, who loved her so deeply that He died for her. In her desperation she accepted this last ray of hope. Had not the blood of pigs and even of her pet dog failed to help? Perhaps the blood of this Man Jesus was the answer.

Kai sang, "Jesus loves me, this I know," and prayed a simple prayer requesting help if it would bring glory to God's name.

The woman was sleeping when Kai left the hut. It was cold and dark outside, so he grasped a burning stick from the fire, which he waved to keep the tip glowing so that he could find his way home. But before he arrived, he heard the cry echo across the marsh, "Mary carry 'im pickaninny finish! God belong Seven Day 'im 'e strong too much." (The woman has given birth to the child. The God of the Seventh-day Adventists is very strong.)

6

Intertribal Warfare

For six years I directed the treatment of lepers at Togoba. We admitted 850 patients and discharged 400. Thus, when transferred to the Omaura mission station in 1955, I handed over to Dr. Roy O. Yeatts 450 patients. The doctor and his wife both gave loving and unstinting service during the years they spent there and at the Sopas Hospital.

At Omaura on the eastern extremity of the highlands we found large villages, a small mission hospital, and a school.

Over the mountains behind the mission one of my devoted assistants, Lamai, ranged in search of those who would accept a better way of life. At Baira, high on a ridge, he found willing listeners. Later accompanying him on a visit there, I found our journey to be the usual test of physical endurance, crossing high mountains, grassy valleys, and swift rivers.

At one point a bridge had been cut by a hostile group during tribal fighting. Heavy rain in the mountains had made the stream a roaring torrent. To go forward was impossible. It was too late to return home.

Energetically the carriers applied tomahawks to the base of a tall casuarina tree which we hoped to use as a bridge. The tree trembled, hesitated, and finally fell across the stream to the far bank. We eyed it cautiously before venturing across. Although the log vibrated as the swirling water tugged at its branches, we were all able to scramble across.

The final ascent was precipitous, but the sun was low and had lost its piercing heat. Soon we reached the ridge and walked

(25)

3—B.T.N.

along it toward Baira village. Below us roared the river, above rose yet higher peaks.

The sun was setting in golden splendor, and as we entered the village and were greeted with spontaneous delight all seemed at peace. That evening as the whole village flocked to worship, I was surprised to hear them lustily sing simple choruses Lamai had taught them.

In the morning the sick gathered. Many had nagging teeth to be extracted, and one even had a cyst to be removed from the ear under local anesthetic. Injections and tablets were given, dressings fastened, and prayers offered for God's healing balm.

During the afternoon friendly but nervous men from the nearby village of Nimbairo sauntered up, armed with fighting bows and arrows. They listened to the Bible stories, and, still holding their weapons, for the first time bowed their heads.

Following worship, as I sat outside my hut listening to the conversation of the people, I saw from the height of this ridge the deep valley that dropped more than a thousand feet and then zoomed up to the majestic heights of Mount Piori, 12,000 feet. This was one of those rare nights when the mountains were clear and the sunset pinks lingered long on the lofty heights.

The two tribes sat tensely apart but gradually relaxed as they talked. First one chief rose, then the other. Both told how they had lived in fear of each other for as long as their forefathers could remember. They were afraid to go hunting unless in armed groups. Their women feared to go to their gardens unless protected by their husbands. Every night they lived in dread of attack. Members of one tribe were continually poisoning members of the other in feudal "pay-backs."

But this day their hearts had been touched by the God of heaven who loves them and wants them to love each other. Would we send them a missionary? they asked. One who would treat their illnesses and teach them how to love instead of hate?

A government patrol had recently been sent to quell fighting between these two tribes. But the tribesmen attacked the patrol as it came down a ridge, and several policemen were wounded. The patrol, however, outflanked the savages and sent them scurrying down the mountainside, leaving thirty-seven shields and hundreds of arrows.

But these hardened warriors would not easily admit defeat. During the night they concealed themselves behind huge boulders and again showered the patrol with arrows. When the sun rose, the Australian officer appealed to them to surrender; but they shouted defiance until he advanced toward them covered by his policemen. As warning bullets spattered the rock where the tribesmen stood, the chief finally capitulated.

But now their hearts were subdued. "We want peace," the chief told me. "Peace with our neighbors and the government, peace with God. Please help us. We do not know how to live peaceably." Again the power of the Word of God was demonstrated, and the two-edged sword proved mightier than guns.

Both sides laid down their weapons before me and promised to follow the mission way of life. One chief pointed to a man, his wife, and their young son. "These are all that are left in one whole village just across the valley." The constant feuding among ferocious fighters had killed all the rest.

Shortly after we sent a married evangelist to Baira. He effected an amazing transformation of the two tribes. Those who formerly stalked each other now walk and worship together.

Our schoolteacher at Omaura was a Massau islander named Tamangie. I asked him if he would like to spend his term-end vacation at Baira village helping to build a church. He readily agreed, but he also requested permission to visit a new tribe over the shoulder of Mount Piora in the Aziana Valley.

I consented reluctantly, as the area was the stronghold of the barbarous Kukukukus, the most feared fighters of New Guinea. But since he felt a responsibility for these people, I knew God would guide and protect him. I assured him that we would be praying for him daily, and I warned him to be particularly careful.

With a pack on his back and a picture roll under his arm, Tamangie set off. In twelve days at Baira, with the willing aid of the villagers, Tamangie constructed the framework of a church. Then his thoughts turned to the Aziana Valley.

Early in the morning he began his journey with a medical orderly. They took a young lad as an interpreter. They crossed a deep gorge, scaled the slopes of Mount Piora, and slept under its shadow. The people of a village here tried to persuade Tamangie not to visit the dreaded Kukukukus. They told how four of their own number had visited there. When these failed to return, eight more were sent to investigate the cause, and they found that the four had been killed. Feigning sorrow for the murders, the treacherous Kukukukus promised compensation and made a feast for the delegation. But when the feasting was nearly over, the Kukukukus savagely attacked their guests. Only one escaped to struggle back and, with serious wounds, tell the sad tale.

But Tamangie would not be intimidated. He believed in the protecting power of the great God above while he was doing His work. This testimony provided an introduction to the gospel story which Tamangie repeated.

A friendly Kukukuku man, not present when the murders were committed, happened to be in this village and offered to take Tamangie over to his people. But as he could not leave early in the morning, Tamangie and his two companions left without him.

Before dawn the two men of God with their young interpreter resumed their trek along the muddy trail and through the heavy mountain mist. By midafternoon they reached the first village and were greeted sullenly by armed men. Not knowing the language well, the evangelists had difficulty explaining the purpose of their visit. The Kukukukus eyed them suspiciously and discussed among themselves what should be done with the intruders. Death appeared imminent.

Just then the man who had met them over the mountain arrived, rushing to Tamangie, throwing his arms around him, and declaring that Tamangie was his friend. He told his tribesmen to listen to Tamangie and to look at his pictures. Without delay the picture roll was held aloft and the wondrous story of God's boundless love was told.

As they listened attentively, the people gradually softened. Captivated by the story of Jesus, they wanted Tamangie to remain with them; but that was impossible. The medical orderly treated those who were suffering from various maladies, further winning the hearts of these Kukukukus. They agreed to give up their murderous ways and be friendly to their neighbors.

Several days later Tamangie and his companions were on the trail once more, recrossing the range with rejoicing hearts. When they arrived in the village where they had been warned against the Kukukukus, the people were amazed to see them, and their admiration for the God of Tamangie was increased.

Taking a shorter route now, the mission party planned to cross the Lamari River and spend the night at Baira village. At about eight o'clock in the morning, while still in Kukukuku country, they reached an unknown village.

As he passed through, Tamangie spoke cheerfully to the glum-faced, unresponding villagers. One of them noticed the wide belt Tamangie was wearing and probably thought he was an unarmed policeman. A few weeks previously a policeman had apprehended one of the villagers for murder, and they were eager for revenge.

"Kill him! Kill him!" they cried, rushing into their huts, the men seizing extra arrows, the women snatching their children and running off into the jungle.

With pounding hearts the three men hastened on, each one praying. Following them along the top of the ridge, the enraged Kukukukus took aim at Tamangie and his friends below. But a man dashed down from the group above and ran toward Tamangie, while the wild mob shouted to him, "Get out of the way! We want to kill the strangers!"

The man raced on, telling Tamangie not to follow the trail or they would be ambushed and killed. He directed them over a fence and across a garden, where they were able to melt into the jungle. Thus they were saved from arrows and certain death.

With tears of gratitude flowing, Tamangie told me of this escape, certain that the one who came to their rescue was a disguised angel.

Now hundreds of the Kukukukus happily fill churches and give glory to God, living proof that perfect love casteth out fear.

7

Moi-Ye

Stationed at a mission outpost on the western slopes of mighty Mount Michael were an intrepid young man named Moi-ye, his wife and two children, and two assistants. The tribesmen at this place had pleaded passionately for help from us, and this group had willingly responded.

The village was situated on a bend of the Tua River where it abruptly changes its southerly course and flows westward. Moi-ye often gazed downstream and wondered about the stories he had heard of the mysterious people dwelling toward the setting of the sun. Did they really live in trees like animals? Did they actually eat their own dead? If so, should they not be told about Jesus? But who would go? He himself?

The thought burned in his mind until finally he made the decision. Sadly Moi-ye bade his wife and children good-bye, for the people he intended to visit were savages. One of his helpers would accompany him; the other was charged with the care of Moi-ye's family during his absence. If Moi-ye did not return within a month, this man was to take the family back to their village; and they were not to mourn for him. Committing his loved ones to God's protection, this apostle to the highland and his friend set their faces westward.

Day after day the two plodded on, sleeping in strange villages and never failing to acquaint the people with the gospel story. In each place they were warned not to venture into the country of the "tree dwellers." But always Moi-ye assured them that he must go on, even at the cost of his life.

At last there loomed ahead the last mountain between them and their destination. The jungle was dense, and bloodsucking leeches tormented them. Hacking their way through the undergrowth, they struggled up to the summit and caught their first glimpse of the unknown Karimui district.

By midafternoon the travelers were passing through primitive gardens, where the people had planted taro, *kau kau,* and bananas between the trunks of felled trees. As the jungle parted, revealing signs of human habitation, Moi-ye and his friend stopped in their tracks and stared at a tall two-story structure. This was the reason these people were called tree dwellers. Their houses were built high off the ground, and in some cases living tree trunks were used as supports.

Suddenly the visitors realized that they had been seen. A wild cry issued from the building, and men appeared at the doorway of the upper floor armed with bows and arrows. Seeing that Moi-ye and his companion were unarmed, the men relaxed a little, cautiously came down the rickety stairway, and approached the missionaries.

"Who are these brave but foolish strangers who came to see us?" asked one.

"What are we going to do with them?" queried another.

"Why not dispose of them as we do with all misguided visitors?" suggested an old man.

As Moi-ye's companion voiced his fears, Moi-ye hung his picture roll on a tree stump. Not having seen such a thing before, the warriors gathered around and were soon intrigued by the pictures and stories.

Could it be possible that there is a God who loves men and does not require appeasement? As the evangelist continued the sweet story of Jesus, sullen looks changed to smiles, evil intentions died, cruel hearts were mellowed by the Holy Spirit, and bows and arrows fell to the ground.

More men appeared. Women and children squatted timidly in the background, enraptured by the pictures and the message.

Then an elderly man near the back started forward. Aware of the crowd's interest, yet fearing a change of mood, Moi-ye watched intently. The man stopped in front of the picture roll, and gazed at the face of Jesus depicted there.

"I have seen this Man's face before," he announced to the people. "The story you have just heard is true. This stranger has come with a message from the great God above, and what he says we must do."

With astonishment Moi-ye and his friend listened to the old man's story. Years before he was one day working in his garden when dark clouds and rumblings of thunder gave warning of a violent outburst of the elements. A brilliant flash of lightning and a deafening crash from the heavens sent him sprawling on the ground in fear. When he regained a little composure, he raised his eyes and saw, serenely looking down at him from the cloud, a face that was strong yet full of compassion. Slowly the picture faded, but not before it had etched itself indelibly upon the old man's mind.

The appealing face had changed the pattern of his whole life. No longer did he join in the heathen rituals or cannibal feasts. He was a man apart, waiting to see more of the face in the cloud.

Immediately Moi-ye was elevated to a place of honor by the men of Karimui. And every day he proclaimed the gospel without fear.

Disease and degradation were everywhere. Lying silently suffering in their huts were people of all ages, some with eroding tropical ulcers devouring their flesh and exposing their bones, providing torment for months and years. Yaws, malaria, scabies, and badly infected injuries were rife. Although not a trained orderly, Moi-ye was able to give elementary treatment, which, combined with his prayers, afforded some relief.

When one of these suffering ones died, his fellow tribesmen ate him. Outside the large hut were platforms on which were drying human bones, the remains of cannibal meals. When dry, these bones were distributed among relatives of the devoured dead and worshiped as symbols of the departed spirits.

As the clans were all mutually suspicious, Moi-ye was prevented from traveling farther on the extensive plateau. He had hoped to visit other tribes, for it was apparent their condition was no better. But now he decided to return home for more help. As he departed, his hosts expressed their sorrow; but Moi-ye assured them he would return.

Great was the joy of Moi-ye's family when he and his companion returned unharmed. But Moi-ye was restless. His heart had been stirred by what he had seen and heard. Never before had a missionary ventured into this stronghold of Satan. Now its defenses had been penetrated and some of its prisoners freed. His mind was continually busy with thoughts of how to help his Karimui friends. When he reported his adventure to me, I decided to visit Karimui.

8

The Walkabout

We laid plans for a six-weeks' expedition, the government anxious that I engage in an anti-yaws campaign, the public health department willingly supplying all required medicine. This meant giving every man, woman, and child an injection of penicillin in oil, a process which would almost eradicate the disfiguring disease in the area.

Then began the task of preparing in detail for the long walkabout. At Goroka we gathered cases of medical supplies, food, and camping equipment packed for the trail. We alerted thirty-five carriers to be ready at the staging point near Lufa, on the western slopes of Mount Michael, at the end of the vehicular road.

Eric Were, an Australian who had spent several years in New Guinea managing a gold mine, now a professional movie producer in Vancouver, Canada, wanted to shoot a film of the glaring need for missions in New Guinea. When he learned of our walkabout, he contacted me.

Since he was a close friend with a venturesome spirit and a sparkling sense of humor, I was delighted to have him join our expedition. He made arrangements with the General Conference of Seventh-day Adventists to sponsor his film, "Cry of New Guinea."

We loaded the Land Rover with medical equipment and supplies, food, clothing, utensils, several fifty-pound bags of rice and salt, buckets, tomahawks, bush knives, and a lightweight tarp that served as an open-ended tent. Leaving our mission home, we drove across the long, flimsy, swaying, cable-suspended Kami River bridge. We afterward learned how fortunate we were, for a few days later the bridge collapsed under another Land Rover, drowning both driver and passenger. Passing Lufa, the last government patrol post, we were increasingly impeded by landslides and fallen rocks until finally, lumbering over the last obstacle, we parked the vehicle on a ridge facing the seemingly endless mountains over which we were to trudge.

Met here in the afternoon by the impatient carriers, at an elevation of 7,000 feet on the mountainside as the cold rain was about to fall, I asked Eric, "What are your thoughts—to start now or tomorrow?"

"I'm easy," he said; "but the mountains will be no smaller tomorrow, so let's get on our way now."

So we unloaded the cargo and distributed it among the carriers, some preferring to carry their loads on poles tied with vines cut from the bush beside the road. With a loud "whoop" from the line we set off. I could not share the exuberance of the carriers, as the trail followed along the steep mountainside, down a deep gorge, and up the other side with rain above and the seemingly eternal mud below. As waterproof coats would be too uncomfortable and clammy for such exertion, we walked soaking wet.

Under these conditions even the carriers' enthusiasm soon waned, but after three hours of endurance we crawled out of a gully and into Megino village.

That night we heated mushroom soup and precooked rice with raisins—a feast. A fruitcake my wife had packed enlarged Eric's eyes despite my grave pronouncement that this luxury was reserved for the furthermost point of our journey. However, after only three days on the rugged trail, the cake had broken into several pieces, making sample bites temptingly easy. Thus, much to Eric's glee, barely a crumb survived the first week.

The first three days on a walkabout seem the hardest, as one continually contrasts his discomfort with homelife. After the third day one accepts the inevitable and establishes a routine.

Rising soon after daybreak, we pack the beds, wash, shave, eat, and then worship with the carriers. At this simple service we "fasim eye" (fasten, or close, eyes). Then we commend ourselves to our watchful Father, who alone knows all the dangers.

Mountain mist swirled around us as we started out the first morning, before us the mysterious Tua River gorge rarely traversed by white men, and the territory of the treacherous Karimui tree dwellers.

Early in the afternoon we arrived at Hegatura village, site of a small Adventist mission station, and were welcomed with enthusiasm. There we gave penicillin injections to all the people, more than a hundred, the beginning of the anti-yaws campaign (which eventually numbered nearly four thousand injections), and Eric began shooting film.

That evening the village crowded into the small mud-surrounded church, and there we enjoyed worship with these simple jungle people. They like to sing of Jesus' love and hear the promises of the heavenly home prepared for the faithful. We learned that fifteen had already renounced heathenism and were preparing for baptism.

By the end of the week we reached Ugagubie village, an untidy line of round huts strung along a ridge. Eric and I settled into the one reserved for visitors, close to the carriers' huts. Our beds consisted of spring steel frames covered with light canvas. We talked ourselves to sleep reviewing the past day and making plans for the next.

Shortly after three o'clock in the morning the still mountain air was shattered by yells which chilled my spine.

"Help! Help! Quick time!"

"What name something?" (What is the trouble?), I yelled back.

No reply.

"Quick, Eric! There's trouble!" I said.

We both sat upright, hearing frantic beatings against the walls of the hut just behind ours. Night attack, I thought.

Scrambling for my flashlight, I knocked it farther away. When I found it, we shouted, "Me fella come!" and dashed around to the back of our hut. People poured out of their huts. Four men were talking hysterically. In the confusion no one could tell us in pidgin English what had happened.

Finally we learned that the four men had been sleeping in one small hut because of the cold and had awakened and stirred the smoldering embers. While they talked, the low door was slowly pushed open and in crept a *tambaran,* a spirit. Before their terrified gaze it grabbed a stick from the fire, waved it in the air, and began to dance furiously, beating them with the burning stick.

Fearing the *tambaran* more than the fire stick, they tried to break through the flimsy walls, making the beating on the walls we had heard.

When I shouted, the *tambaran* vanished and the men rushed outside. What they had seen had filled them with abject terror. Their worship of the spirits of departed ancestors makes them susceptible to spiritistic visitations. They interpreted this one to mean that someone had died in their village that night, but later investigation proved this fear false.

I believe this manifestation was an attempt by the enemy of souls to intimidate the carriers so that we could not continue.

The ire of the serpent had been displayed, and we saw first-hand that he would not yield his victims without a fight. How close he actually did come to wrecking our walkabout we soon learned.

9

Among the Cannibals

Mile after weary mile we struggled up and over mountains and waded across the flooded torrents in the valleys, stopping at each village to open the medical case. Always after administering treatments we unrolled the pictures and spoke to a receptive audience.

People suffered silently with such diseases as pneumonia, eventually to die, when a series of injections would have saved them. Others were tormented with malaria, head and bones aching, the whole body burning, when tablets would have driven the malady out. At one village alone five had recently died.

Tropical ulcers were perhaps the greatest cause of suffering. Untreated, these painful sores sometimes eat through skin, muscle, and blood vessels to attack the bone and persist for years. On the leg of one woman was a twelve-inch ulcer and its accompanying scar. In this condition she had given birth to a child now four years old.

What would the critics of missions say if they could see the unrelieved suffering as we have seen it in these remote parts of New Guinea? Would they themselves be able to turn away from the eyes of a mother as she brings her dying child and begs for help?

The village of Manie was pleasantly situated on a spur pointing toward the deep Tua River gorge below, with its mantle of dark purple. The people gave us an animated reception.

For several hours Robebe, the orderly, and I gave injections and many other treatments. These seemed particularly happy people, appreciative, and anxious to learn all we could teach them about the "big fella Papa on top."

Before we left in the morning the chief, in an eloquent appeal for a missionary, began waving his arm around and saying we could select any ground, even the choicest garden, for a mission site. We had helped his people in their suffering, and he wanted his people to learn more about our God of love.

A few days previously a young man had died. The villagers placed his body covered with tree bark on a high platform next to a hut still inhabited. His most valued treasure, a red loin-cloth, was placed on the platform with the body, to rot.

As we trekked deeper into the mysterious hinterland and approached the land of the Karimui cannibals, our carriers became restive. When we reached the last village before crossing the mountains into the Karimui country, the local chief, meaning to be helpful, told the carriers it was suicidal to venture any farther. If we were not all killed by arrows, he said, we would be poisoned. Most of the carriers were not Christians and were susceptible to the chief's apprehensions, especially after the *tambaran* experience a few nights earlier.

Our dependable guide, Moses, advised us against continuing into Karimui, requesting Eric to influence me not to proceed. We both smiled, realizing his efforts could have been as much for his own safety as ours, but still grateful for his consideration. While he knew the cruelty of the unconverted heathen, we knew the power of our Protector.

Departing the following morning in a depressing but short-lived rain, we found the upward route very steep, with no true trail. Slimy leeches attached themselves to us as we passed, clinging tenaciously, sucking our blood, as we continually dragged them from our limbs.

The mountain mists dispersed just after midday, the jungle parted, and the Karimui plateau, the dreaded land, came into view. Dominated by a camel-humped mountain, with its mantle of thick jungle bordered by a loop of the Tua River, this large plateau looked deceptively flat.

Beginning at the relatively level base of the steep mountain, we climbed for two hours before reaching the first big dwelling. Upon seeing Moi-ye, the occupants relaxed and received us gaily. The carriers cut small trees and banana leaves and made rough huts for themselves. We hung our tarp over a ridgepole, spread it apart, and tied its edges to stakes. For several weeks this was our shelter and the earth our floor.

We were fascinated by these strange people. Their two-story dwellings were sixty to eighty feet long and about twenty feet wide. The first floor was ten feet off the ground, and here the women and children slept with the small pigs. The women cooked food and passed it through holes in the ceiling to the men above. In the second story were cubicles about ten by eight feet, in each of which several men slept. The men spent most of their time smoking locally grown tobacco. They used pipes made from eighteen-inch lengths of bamboo with a hole drilled near the blocked ends for the insertion of tobacco rolled in dried tree leaves.

Access to the dwellings was gained by climbing up crude ladders. On the approach of an enemy these were drawn into the huts, and the men would shoot arrows from above. The filth of these houses both inside and out nauseates the stomach and boggles the mind. Scraps of food spat on the floor were never removed. There was no form of sanitation whatsoever.

A whole clan lived in each house, perhaps for collective protection. Whenever a person died, a supporting post in the cubicle where he had lived was cut. Thus, after a number of deaths, the large structure became unsafe and was abandoned. In case of an epidemic such as dysentery, when several deaths could occur in a short time, the occupants would have to vacate promptly. In this way they no doubt left behind most of their source of infection, deriving some benefit from their apparent folly.

Making the vicinity of this first dwelling our base for two days, we treated the many sick people—people who until then had had absolutely no medical aid. We gave injections for their hideous sores and applied dressings. One young man who was near death with malaria was carried piggyback to us and responded slowly to treatment. That same day a man had been struck on the head with a tomahawk following a dispute over a girl. We sewed up the gash, though we feared a depressed skull fracture.

The next day we walked to two distant houses, returning to camp at night. At the first one the people refused to gather for injections, saying their chief had died. To make sure their excuse was genuine, I asked to see the body, but they made further excuses. Then, apparently anxious to placate me, they brought a finger freshly cut off a body. We could only guess that the body was being eaten.

During the night the friendly chief near our camp had told our carriers not to cross the Sena River or they would never return. We planned to patrol through the whole area, and we needed loyal carriers.

But discontent seemed to grow among the non-Christian carriers, so I decided to bring the matter to a climax. I told all the carriers that, in spite of the chief, I intended to go on. I said that I believed God would care for us as long as we did His bidding and that I was not afraid myself, but that I did not want any frightened men to discourage the others. All who wished could return over the mountain and wait for us. There was silence; no one moved. I pointed to the main murmurer and asked him to come forward, which he did. Then I urged all who had fears to join him.

Slowly one and then another joined the line until I began to wonder if all would desert us. I remarked to Eric that perhaps we would have to go on alone! But fortunately half the line remained.

We needed men to carry the medical supplies, food, and photographic equipment, but by leaving some goods at the base we could manage with those who remained. As it turned out, if all had come we would not have been able to obtain sufficient food. Thus this separation turned out to be a blessing.

So with seventeen loyal men we went forward. Our first obstacle was the bridgeless Sena River. It was too deep to wade,

and the carriers, mountain men, were unable to swim. Eric un-
packed his equipment and took movie footage while we
searched the jungle for long, strong rattan cane, which we
stretched over the water and tied to a tree. Using this as a safety
line, we slowly but surely shepherded the supplies and carriers
over to the other side. One plucky man with our bedding tried
to wade across unassisted, but was swept off his feet. Seeing
him and our bedding bobbing downstream, we quickly sprang
into action and managed after a few nervous minutes to retrieve
both.

Just across the river was a typical house, in front of which
were bones, evidence of cannibalism, bleaching in the sun. As
we photographed the bones and examined them, the people
regarded us sullenly. Then we saw a platform of bones, all devoid of flesh except the feet. Upon investigating these remains, I
found evidence of disease, advanced yaws in one and a bad
tropical ulcer in the other.

After some humoring, the people eventually lined up for injections, although the men continued to puff nervously on their
bamboo pipes. As timid as jungle animals, the women peered
from behind capes of beaten bark. We filled the sterilized sy-
ringes and started giving the "shoots," Robebe at one end of the
line, I at the other. Ten minutes later he rushed up to me and
whispered, "Come lookim one fella Mary. 'Im 'e got leg belong
man along neck belong 'im." (Come and see a woman with a
man's foot around her neck.)

"This," I remarked to Eric, "is going to be interesting. Come
and see what it is all about."

We got a picture of it, the dried skin of a man's foot tied
around a woman's neck. Was this grisly object a charm, a sign of
sorrow for the dead, an act of penance, or merely a decoration?
The wearer showed no embarrassment when we looked at it, a
revolting sight to us, but not glaringly gruesome in the local
setting.

Continuing our journey, we met a group along the trail who
seemed half expecting us. Apparently they had heard that we
were bringing the white man's magical "shoots," for when re-

quested they willingly lined up. We hoped they would also learn to value God's supreme gift of salvation, and offered a prayer.

At the next village we met a tribe who not many months before had raided another tribe around the mountain, killing their chief, whose body was trussed on a pole, carried triumphantly home, and amidst great festivity, cooked and eaten. However, they received us kindly, and showed evidence that they were thirsting for something better. It was a joy to bring these simple people satisfying draughts of living water from the fountain of everlasting life and to minister to their bodily ailments. Hearts were convicted, and later a bountiful harvest was gathered here.

10

"Why Are My People Dying?"

From the perpetual mud came tiny jungle flies that plagued us day and night, their bites like jabs from a red-hot needle. The mesh of our mosquito nets was not fine enough to keep them out. In order to sleep we were often forced to cover our heads with towels.

On the Karimui plateau, wherever there was or had been a garden, fallen logs made the pathways, often wet and covered with moss. For the barefoot highlanders this was not the problem it was for us in our boots, containing many fewer spikes than when we started. Crossing single-log bridges over gullies was the most dangerous even with the aid of our surefooted friends. At times, to avoid a slip which would have meant a fall of up to fifty feet, we crawled across on hands and knees in a most undignified manner, much to the mirth of the carriers. Even so, Eric and I more than once slipped and crashed into the undergrowth.

Besides the ever-present mud and rotting rubbish we smelled the sickly sweet odor of human flesh drying on the bones in the sun. The only domestic animal was the filthy pig, which lived with the people on the same level, equally at home. Such was the setting for cannibalism.

For offensiveness no village equaled Diwei, where on the second day the chief asked me, "Why are my people dying?" The answer was so obvious that at first I was bewildered. Why indeed! I pointed out to him the pollution surrounding his hut and the habit of devouring the dead. This was not the way the true God intended human beings to live. He who created man expected him to live on a high plane. The worship of Kora only degraded them, I explained, but the worship of God in heaven would lift them up.

The chief listened thoughtfully and then implored, "Please, won't you help us? We have observed that you live a better life, and we want someone to teach us." This required a staff and a staff required transportation, but I promised to help as soon as we could.

While examining this clan of seventy-eight members the first day, I was amazed to find fourteen lepers—a staggering 18 percent, when a 3 percent incidence is considered high. (Upon completing this medical walkabout I reported to the director of public health an incredibly high overall leprosy incidence of 10 percent in Karimui and suggested that the director send the leprologist to investigate. When I later accompanied the leprologist to Karimui, he found to his amazement just over a 10 percent incidence of this disease.

Into Diwei was carried a miserably thin twelve-year-oid girl suffering from a large ulcer caused by yaws. The ulcer completely encircled her ankle. We treated her for the duration of our stay, and we learned later that she had completely recovered.

In another case a man carried his wife to us piggyback. Two of her toes had been eaten away. In spite of their shocking degradation this man's solicitude for his wife was touching.

Seeing the pitiful condition of these people, I was able better to appreciate Christ's feeling when he saw the multitudes: "He was moved with compassion" for them. In the two days we spent here we shared the consolation of Christ with these suffering people and felt bound closely to them. Some time later we were able to send them a national missionary, and now there is a clean mission station in Dewei.

Passing an almost deserted village the following day, we saw a woman holding a badly burned child. The whole side of his face was covered with a suppurating black scab and one eye was swollen and badly infected. The child had rolled into the fire days before, and the only "medicine" these people used was ashes, which his mother had rubbed into the oozing wound.

Rain was falling at the time, so we quickly dressed the injuries with acriflavine emulsion, gave the little mite an injection of penicillin in oil, and offered a prayer. When returning along this route a little more than a week later, I thought to give the little patient another treatment. Arriving at the hut we asked for his mother and were told that she was away in her garden. We asked and were told that the child's face and head were healed. This we could not believe; so we insisted that we see him. Eventually we tired of waiting and were just setting off when a woman came along the trail. We had almost passed her when I suddenly recognized the mother and child we were looking for. The bandage was gone, and clean, healthy flesh covered the whole burned area. His once swollen eye was clear and fully open.

"A miracle!" exclaimed Eric. Though the mother was shy, we could see she was decidedly happier, and the little boy smiled contentedly.

After twenty-four days of arduous slogging over mountains and through mud, we reached the end of our trek. We had crossed into Papua to visit the last of the Karimui people. During the last two days the language had abruptly changed. When entering any new language area, I always asked the name of the local god or spirit. In the first part of Karimui the people worshipped Kora, but here the god was called Kebe-eberie, a name which rather intrigued us.

As we trudged along, a local man suggested we turn aside and look at a river that disappeared into the ground. Apparently it was a huge stream at times, but only a trickle was running this day. We followed the stream to a limestone hill where it plunged down and disappeared into a yawning cavern. Outside the entrance was a jumble of rocks and tree trunks that had been washed down when the river was in flood.

Standing at the entrance to the cave, I remarked to the carriers, "Me think this fella place 'im 'e headquarters belong Kebe-eberie." No sooner had I finished speaking than an eerie swoosh, swoosh, swoosh emanated from the dark depths of the cave. If I had had hair on my head, I am sure it would have stood on end. I even thought I could see the boys' tightly curled hair struggling to unwind.

For a few seconds we were shocked into silence; then someone said, "Me think big fella black bokis 'im 'e walkabout inside." (I think there is a flying fox flapping about inside.) We all burst out laughing, and it seemed wiser to accept this explanation.

Returning home along the same route we had come, we were met by several chiefs. They repeated their plaintive pleas for help. I was anxious to help, but these people were too remote. Being a pilot, my mind naturally turned to a mission aircraft and the possibility of an airstrip in a central situation as a solution. To fly would take only twenty-five minutes from Goroka, in contrast with one week of arduous walking. After landing at a central point, a day or so walking east or west would bring us to any village.

Fortunately the government intended to construct an airstrip, and my medical report on conditions in the Karimui district served to strengthen these intentions. A level site had already been selected by an administration patrol officer, so I encouraged the natives to plant larger gardens and prepare to help the government. This they did, and a light-aircraft landing field which was constructed some time later greatly expanded our mission program.

On this walkabout I met the son of the man who had seen the face of Jesus in the clouds. He had now become chief and a champion of the gospel, anxious to lead his people into the light that had shone upon his father from the heavens. Before we parted, he begged me to return. In fact, he said he would allow me three months—one month to go home, one month to prepare, and one month to return with my wife!

Eric had compiled what was to me a thrilling record of the needs of the mission field on film, operating his cameras in humidity, dirt, and appalling conditions that would have quickly disheartened a lesser man.

Feeling now like hardened jungle dwellers, we finally dragged our aching limbs up the last ridge and stood at the end of the vehicular road, from which point the Land Rover would take us effortlessly home. In six weeks we had walked three hundred miles over mountains and through mud and had administered thousands of injections and other treatments. Both leaner for the trip, we felt more than compensated for the privations of the long trek by the satisfaction of having helped the helpless.

11

Challenging Kora and Kebe-Eberie

Shortly after the Karimui walkabout, I met with my national evangelists in what amounted to a council of war. "Should we leave the supremacy of Kora and Kebe-eberie unchallenged in the gloom of Karimui?" I asked.

Moi-ye volunteered to set up an outpost at the last village before crossing into Karimui. We promised to obtain medical supplies for him to use on forays into Karimui from his base. We felt this was the best we could do until an airstrip was built there.

After settling into his new environment, Moi-ye visited the surrounding villages with medicine and the picture roll. By practicing the healing art and preaching the gospel he succeeded in turning many from worshiping evil spirits to serving the Creator.

One afternoon as he was visiting a nearby tribe watching the women removing food from the hot stones in the pit where, covered with leaves and earth, it had been cooking, Moi-ye saw the teeth of a human head leering up at him.

He reprimanded the people, saying that cannibalism was a great evil. He discovered that this was the third diseased body that had been eaten in the last five days. The people could say only that human flesh tasted sweeter than pig. The patrol officer at Lufa, on receiving a report of this incident, investigated and apprehended the main offenders, nineteen women. I believe cannibalism is practiced in New Guinea primarily for ritualistic reasons; it soon dies out when people accept Christianity or are pressured from the government.

Acting with typical dispatch in the case of a proven need, the government, a year later, hacked an airstrip out of the jungle on the Karimui plateau. This airstrip was opened, providing twenty-five minutes flying time against one week of hard slogging on the track.

I lost no time flying an orderly to Karimui, and the people, heartened by our presence, willingly helped build their own clinic and field hospital. Not having a mission plane, we chartered commercial aircraft. I flew in regularly to assist the orderly and other workers posted there. Serious medical cases could now be quickly and easily flown to Goroka and placed under expert medical care.

Wishing to see the notorious Karimui people, my wife Mavis and my daughter flew with me on one of my trips, staying near our medical post at the airstrip while I spent two weeks visiting our growing number of stations.

One morning while strolling around the mission station, Mavis noticed a woman sitting beside the pathway, in the local fashion, naked except for a drape hanging from her waist back and front and holding a string bag, or *biloom,* which hangs from the forehead down the back. Inside the *biloom* was a tiny baby cradled in green leaf diapers. She stopped beside the woman, indicating that she would like to see the baby. Proudly the mother opened the *biloom,* pushed aside the leaves, and lifted the infant.

With a little encouragement from Mavis, the baby, much to the mother's delight, was soon smiling. Although they could not speak one intelligible word to each other, the warm bond of motherhood drew them together. When the little mite attempted to grasp Mavis's hand, she was shocked to see a swollen and inflamed stump instead of a finger. She tried to express sympathy, but the mother only continued to smile and talk in her own tongue. Mavis pointed to the clinic and suggested as best she could that the child be taken to the clinic and have the tiny finger stump dressed. The mother did not move.

Bewildered, Mavis called an interpreter, who repeated her suggestions. Still the mother was unperturbed. So Mavis asked how the injury had occurred. The young mother had bitten the finger off herself, explaining that she did this because her two other children had died and she hoped this action would prevent her losing this one.

On this walkabout we intended to give the people further spiritual and medical help, assess their needs, and select sites for additional mission outposts. Thankfully we found somewhat less illness this time.

Arriving at Maino village the second Friday afternoon, we received a rousing reception. The three local chiefs had built two huts in anticipation of our coming. As we came in sight, the leading chief dashed down the trail to greet me shouting, *"Abagie! Abagie!"* I discovered that this word means "friend."

Attending to medical work in the morning, I noted that since our initial patrol the people were at least a little cleaner and fewer were sick. As we opened the picture roll, the lisping tongues of these savages repeated the name of Jesus, and their ears listened with keen attention to our messages of the riches of Christ.

A picture of Kebe-eberie (the devil) being defeated by Jesus the Conqueror, brought hope. And the story of the wonderful place called heaven seemed to thrill them beyond my power to describe. Could it be possible, they asked, that Jesus would help them reach this place? I assured them that indeed He would, and at the close of the service many of them raised hands when asked who wanted to go there.

That afternoon the three leaders came to talk. They said they were very grateful. Already they were healthier. Our God must be superior to Kebe-eberie, or we would not have been able to help them as we had. Then came the expected plea for a Christian teacher. I was perplexed, knowing we could not find enough evangelists, but at the same time unwilling to disappoint these chiefs when their need was so apparent and their appeal so earnest.

Suddenly two of the chiefs seized two of the carriers by the arms and jumped up and down shouting *"Abagie! Abagie!"* as they thumped the ground. These two men could be their missionaries, they begged. Each could have one of the two huts already built. The men of the village would shoot cassowaries—large, flightless, dangerous birds, locally considered a great delicacy—and other birds for them to eat. Before, their people were dying; now their life expectancy had increased, and the power of Kebe-eberie had been broken. Holding his abdomen, one of the chiefs exclaimed, "Story belong Jesus sweet too much along bel belong me." (The story of Jesus is delicious to me.)

I prayed about the matter, then I told the chiefs we would send someone as soon as possible. Some time later we were able to fulfill our promise.

The next morning we struggled along the slushy track once more, crossing streams, crawling along slippery logs, and tripping over tree roots. Shortly after midday someone at the rear of the line of carriers shrieked, "One fella man 'im 'e fall down, now 'im 'e die finish." A man had fallen down and died, a panting messenger told me. Hurrying back, I saw one of the men writhing on the ground, frothing and bleeding at the mouth. To all appearances he was dying. However, an examination revealed that he was suffering an epileptic fit, and the blood had come from his bitten tongue. He was one of the two whom the chiefs had grabbed the previous day; apparently he had been badly shocked, imagining the worst.

Using tomahawks and knives, the carriers made a stretcher from poles and bark, and four willing lads transported their companion until we came to the first stream, little more than a trickle, but with banks ten feet high and covered with tangled roots and vines. Carrying the stretcher across this obstacle was impossible, so we threw it away, and the men took turns carrying him piggyback, struggling for two and a half hours through the jungle, crossing small gullies where we had to decide whether to risk the slippery log that served as a bridge or to chance the steep gully sides. Late that afternoon they wearily stumbled into camp, the sick man still clinging weakly to his helper.

I thought of the poem by Linda Hanbury:

So we thank you, Fuzzy-wuzzies,
for all that you have done,
Not only for Australia, but
for every mother's son;
And we're glad to call you friends,
though your color may be black,
For we know that Christ walked
with you on the Owen Stanley Track.

Upon returning to headquarters I selected several stronger workers to man the difficult posts among these cannibals. Calling the churches together for a special meeting, I threw out the challenge of Karimui to them, and several young men volunteered to unite with the experienced workers there.

After the airstrip was opened, Moi-ye and his family moved into the tribe whose chief had seen the face of Jesus in the clouds. The group responded to his message and soon built new huts, one for each family unit. Sanitation and hygiene were organized, a commodious church arose on the site of the long community dwelling, and in place of the mournful dirge for the departed there was the joyful praise to the God above the clouds. And instead of the bones of cannibal feasts drying in the sun there were platforms heaped with tithe from the gardens.

At the mission outpost adjacent to the airstrip we stationed Odo, a trained orderly, to give medical care. The local chief had a son about nine years of age, and both regularly attended worship services. When the boy became sick, Odo treated him as an outpatient; and when he stopped coming for medicine, Odo presumed he had recovered. But in fact his mother had refused to allow him to receive medicine, administering her own concoctions until the worsening boy died.

Three days later Odo and Paul, another orderly, heard of the boy's death and went to visit the parents. Inside the hut a group of hysterical women relatives were wailing loudly and caressing the body. When Odo asked the mother if they could bury the body, she and the other relatives objected noisily.

The following day the orderlies returned with a coffin made from a medicine case lined with bandage material. The stench of the body was intolerable; and the women, devoid of reason, refused to allow the men to place the body in the makeshift coffin. Revolted, Odo fled the hut violently sick.

Determined to do their duty, the two men returned on the fifth day with the coffin and several other people. It was useless to reason any more; so, ignoring the objecting women, Odo and Paul placed the boy's remains in the casket.

Burying the dead was a strange new custom to the villagers who gathered to witness. The chief looked on while Sokuwa and several helpers dug his son's grave. Using a picture roll depicting the second coming of Christ, Odo spoke animatedly of the resurrection of the dead, particularly stirring to the father. The boy's body was buried in the family garden at the father's request, for here the lad had loved to play while his father worked. The chief, tired of the depravity of heathenism and longing for peace and security, wanted to see his son again above anything else.

Following Odo's description of the resurrection, the chief confessed with tears his belief in Jesus' power to give life. Would Odo give him the picture roll so that he could hang it in his hut? He could look at it daily and pray to the Giver of life.

Thus the first Christian burial was carried out in this area so long ruled by the powers of darkness. Today Christian interment is customary. These people no longer cringe in fear at the mention of the evil spirits Kora and Kebe-eberie. The gloom of cannibalism has given place to the glow of a celestial light, and they exclaim, "Truly the light is sweet."

Leading the party who dug the first grave in Karimui was Sokuwa, the man who had volunteered to accompany Moi-ye on his initial journey here. When Moi-ye moved to the fringe of the Karimui plateau, it was Sokuwa who had accompanied him and had helped him build the new station. Then Sokuwa offered to move with Moi-ye and his family into Karimui, where for months he toiled until another mission station arose in the jungle.

When Odo was sent to set up a new clinic, it was Sokuwa who faithfully worked with him until the structure was completed. He received no regular pay but was supplied with clothing and soap. His reward was in seeing the gospel change the lives of these desperately needy people and in watching the sick recover their health.

On one of my visits to Karimui, Odo told me that Sokuwa was sick and that his gums would not stop bleeding. Examining Sokuwa, I discovered that he was extremely anemic.

It nearly broke his heart when I told him he would have to go to Goroka with me. He did not want to leave the people and the work he loved so deeply. In the plane Sokuwa was pensive for a while; then, with tears in his eyes, he said, "Me no run away along work belong God. Behind sick 'e finish me like go back along Karimui." (I am not running away from God's work. When I am well I want to return to Karimui.)

But this was not to be. Shortly afterward he died of leukemia, awaiting the voice of his Saviour, "Well done, thou good and faithful servant: . . . enter thou into the joy of thy Lord."

Slowly the number of mission stations increased in the area, including two medical clinics with wide-ranging staff. Tropical ulcers and yaws were almost eradicated after a few months, but malaria, the killer, was there; and leprosy, the crippler, was there.

12

Kinivie, the Killer

"Me like stop along mission," requested Kinivie, the dreaded heathen sorcerer, when I was stationed at Homu. His coming to live on the mission compound was for him the end of a long road of revengeful lust and the beginning of a bright new life.

Until recently, Kinivie had been the terror of the surrounding area. A few pigs or shells were sufficient to bribe him to kill anyone's real or imagined enemies. This was sometimes done by sorcery, when something belonging to the prospective victim was brought to Kinivie. After elaborate incantations and rituals, "poison" was made against the victim, who usually died.

Direct methods of murder he also used. With lowered eyes, Kinivie now told how he would pursue his victims at night with bow and arrow or spear. Stalking them like a ballet dancer performing a dance of death, he would walk on the tips of his toes to confuse his trackers. He waylaid and killed many an unsuspecting person.

As our missionaries advanced into this district, Kinivie dreamed several troubling dreams, each with a recurring theme—the Son of the great God above the clouds was coming back to this earth to save all who faithfully followed Him. In one dream which particularly filled him with terror, he was surrounded by fire with no possibility of escape. He expected to be consumed, but only the tips of his fingers, toes, ears, and nose were burned.

Trembling with fear as he lay on the ground, Kinivie was troubled to know what the dream meant. At this moment a

(56)

bright being approached and, raising him up by the hand, told him that he must prepare for the coming of the great King Jesus.

At this time the incurable disease kuru was making repeated inroads on Kinivie's family. His wife and one daughter had died, and now his only remaining child, an eleven-year-old daughter, the joy of his life, was smitten.

So it was a brokenhearted sorcerer who came to the mission requesting refuge, convinced that his past evil ways were the reason for his calamities and believing these were just retribution. Now he wanted to learn all that this Man Jesus had taught when He was on earth. Then he would go back to his village to follow this wonderful Jesus, to win as many people as he had killed, and to prepare them for His coming.

Sorcery is common in New Guinea, and it takes many forms. To these heathen who have no knowledge of germs, a person never dies from disease. To them death is caused by a member of an enemy tribe. The problem is then to find the guilty one. Lomdopa, the son of a sorcerer and heir to his father's trade, told me some of the methods sorcerers use to discover the supposed wrongdoer.

The corpse is wrapped in pandanus leaves or bark and placed on a platform supported by four poles approximately five feet high. At night several men wait silently nearby until a dull light is seen over the body. A chosen man walks to the platform and taps a post calling each time the name of a suspected culprit. When the right name is called, the body shakes violently, and four men rush forward and hold the posts to prevent the body from falling. The man thus condemned is marked for death.

In another method a man sits atop a hut and sings out to the spirits in a low mystical voice. Other men are posted among the huts of the enemy tribe to watch. After some time the spirit appears in the form of a dull light. The man on the hut calls for an arrow with a burning point, which he shoots into the air. Mysteriously, the light sweeps swiftly back and forth across the sky while the arrow falls harmlessly to the ground nearby. Suddenly the light shoots downward and alights upon the victim's hut, lingering briefly. The spies hiding among the huts carry the news back to the village, and preparations are made to destroy the man whose hut was indicated by the spirit.

To these men this system is rational; they believe that it ensures their survival. To them if one killing is not avenged, the enemy may become emboldened and eventually kill the entire tribe. Although, theoretically, education should help these primitive people understand and explain the relationship between disease and death, as a Christian medical doctor I have found in practice that the simple gospel provides the only full and complete antidote for the lustful killings between tribes.

"Please, sir, one fella Mary die, finish! [Sir, a girl has died!]" gasped a breathless New Guinean one day. According to his story, Seba, who lived a mile away, had fastened a piece of bush twine around her neck and had jumped from a high tree. Finding her lying on the ground, this relative had rushed to tell me what had happened. I had started to console him, when he casually remarked " 'Im 'e no die finish yet. 'Im 'e pullim wind lik lik." (She is not dead yet. She is still breathing a little.)

Chiding him for not telling me this earlier, I rushed to the clinic for an ampoule of adrenalin and a sterile syringe. Then we jumped into the Land Rover, and in a few minutes we were beside the unconscious girl. Her pulse was barely perceptible. An injection and artificial respiration slightly improved her condition, and we were able to take her to the mission station. Twenty-four hours later Seba regained consciousness. Slowly opening her eyes, she smiled wanly. Later she told me this story:

At Sabbath School and church services Seba had learned to love the Lord and had wanted to be baptized, and so she joined the instruction class. When her foster father learned of this he forbade her to attend, citing as a reason her duty to look after his pigs. But she continued attending as before. When she refused to look after the pigs, an integral part of heathenism, the man beat her. Following one particularly violent outburst from her foster father, Seba became utterly discouraged and felt there was no way out of her dilemma except suicide.

Fastening a rope to her neck, she climbed a tree and tied one end near the top. Then she closed her eyes and prayed. Upon opening her eyes, Seba saw three bright beings walking down the road from the mission, one suddenly beginning to run toward her.

She felt she must jump quickly, before anyone reached her. Fortunately the small rope broke as she fell to the ground. Some time later the relative found her lying face downward and came running to inform me.

Sometimes I am asked whether the simple, uneducated people of New Guinea know what Christianity is all about when they are admitted to the church. I reply that I think their commitment to the Lord is sometimes deeper than our own, who have the advantage of an education and the ability to read the Holy Scriptures.

If lack of education were a bar to understanding the essential points of salvation, many precious souls in New Guinea would miss the road to heaven. But when such a simple person accepts Jesus as Lord and Master, it means an involvement of every detail of his life, as illustrated by the following story:

Occasionally my wife would accompany me on a walkabout. On one such patrol a lovable elderly woman decided to help my wife along the way. We had traveled all the morning and had just crossed a narrow log used as a bridge over a stream, when the trail started to climb steeply. Being hot and weary, this dear soul, still leading my wife by the hand, said to her, "Fast 'im eye." (Close your eyes.) Then she offered a short prayer in her own dialect and continued to climb. To her, prayer was as natural as drinking water, and as refreshing.

The dreaded killer kuru, a brain-degenerating disease, claims women victims. It was found only in one area of New Guinea which included a section of Mount Michael. It affects whole tribes and so far has baffled the scientists. The disease brings on a lethargy, followed by a shaking eventually becoming so violent that the victim struggles to walk and eat. Finally paralysis sets in, and, after about twelve months, death ensues.

In the months following our first walkabout, hundreds began

to prepare for baptism, including, in Husa village, a young woman who had just given birth to a child. Then she developed kuru.

At her baptism she was shaking violently and had to be helped down to the stream. Pastor Salau, the officiating minister, had extreme difficulty immersing her. Each time she was lowered to the water, an involuntary spasm of her muscles caused her to leap backward. Finally the rite was accomplished, and for a moment she stood with face upturned toward heaven. Four months later the young woman died, but strong in the hope of the resurrection and entrance into the land of eternal delights.

13

The Fireproof Bible

The words "Go west, young man; go west!" could well be applied to our mission program in the highlands of New Guinea in 1962.

Beginning on the coast at Lae, the long, sinuous road to the highlands crawls up and down the mighty mountain ranges, sometimes slashed by landslides and raging torrents. Creeping up the Kassam Pass to the highlands, it passes close to several Adventist mission stations, including Omaura, Kainantu (the Mount Michael road branching to the left), Bena Bena, and, about two hundred miles from the coast and a little more than five thousand feet in altitude, Goroka, home of the Eastern Highlands Mission headquarters, and, seven miles away, Kabiufa Missionary College.

After gaining Dalo Pass at 8,500 feet, the road dips down to densely populated Chimbu Valley, whose people are famous for their gaudy bird-of-paradise headdresses. To the left are turnoffs to the Yani and Moruma mission stations; then the mountain steeps give way to the fertile flats of the Wahgi Valley. At the end of this valley is Mount Hagen, three hundred fifty miles from Lae and the headquarters of the Western Highlands Mission.

Passing through the leper colony at Togoba, the road labors up to an altitude of 9,000 feet across the Tomba Pass and then drops abruptly into Wabag Valley, the location of Bakamanda Mission. After passing through Wabag with its undulating airstrip it goes on to our modern hospital at Sopas. The road finally descends into the less pretentious valley of Laiagam, 450 tedious miles from the coast. This was to be my base for the next few years.

But the greatest stimulus lay westward. There, where no roads penetrated, tortured mountains and valleys concealed mysterious tribes yet to hear the gospel.

In the words of the great Christian writer, Ellen G. White, "In all the dark corners of the earth, God has in reserve a firmament of chosen ones that will yet shine forth amidst the darkness." I would search the dark corners of these sparsely populated mountains and valleys for such chosen ones.

Notorious for his fighting prowess in the Laiagam Valley before the white man came was Piari. His original name was Armos; but when his fame as a warrior spread, his proud parents changed it to Piari, which means a man strong in battle.

Believing his power came from Timango, the local spirit god who was revered in the form of a sacred stone, Piari and the tribal leaders would pour oblations of pig's blood over the holy stone. And before engaging in a fight they would entreat the god for victory over their enemies. But we later learned that this lustful life had brought no peace to Piari.

When missionaries entered his valley, a curious Piari attended worship with other villagers. Across the mountain in the next valley was another mission operated by the "Seven Days." Still seeking peace of mind, he went to visit them. At the mission he was greeted as a friend and was persuaded to stay there for several weeks.

During this time Piari accepted as truth that which came directly from an amazing Book called the Bible, which contained talk from God himself. At last he found the peace he was seeking and requested the Seventh-day Adventist mission to build a house of worship in his valley.

Pastor J. H. Newman told him there was no one to send. But Piari persisted with his appeal until Pastor Newman said that a man who had been on the mission station for one year could go back with him. Later, he would be replaced by someone with more training.

When Piari and his helper arrived in Laiagam, they were not received with favor. The village men voiced their opposition: "This fella mission no can allow 'im you me along kai kai pig, no pullim smoke. More better you kissim this fella boy he go along other fella half now start 'im mission. (This mission will not let us eat pig or smoke our pipes. It would be better if you took this mission boy to start a station somewhere else.) Piari replied that no one would stop them eating pig or smoking tobacco if they wished to do these things. But as far as he was concerned, he had finished with them.

The old men scowled as they watched Piari and his helper gather bush timber and start erecting a hut. Though they received some help, the work progressed slowly. The posts had to be carried from the mountain above the village, and the grass for thatching had to be cut in the adjacent valley. Finally a modest hut stood in the center of the mission plot.

Several weeks later Piari's helper returned to the base at Rakamanda to report progress and obtain a precious handful of extra nails. One afternoon during his absence Piari was in his garden some distance away when he heard the cry, "Fire! Fire!" and saw flames rising from their hut.

Yelling excitedly, he rushed to the rescue, but too late. As the fire died down, Piari picked up a stick and began to poke among the ashes. The stick struck something solid, his valued Bible. To his amazement and delight, not one page was burned, nor was the cover damaged. "This fella Book," he exclaimed, "'im 'e talk talk belong true fella God on top!" (This book speaks for the true God in heaven!)

Astonished, his neighbors examined the incredible Book that had been preserved from the fire. Scowls changed to expressions of enlightenment. The old men admitted that perhaps there was something special about this Book and its Author who was able to save it.

This incident was a landmark in Piari's life. Piari the fighter became Paul the preacher, and as the years passed I knew no other advocate of the Bible so powerful as Paul Piari. Now his enemy was error and his weapon the Bible.

Paul rebuilt the hut and constructed a small church, which someone also burned one night. Once again the men dragged posts and poles to the site while the women gathered the grass for thatching. After months of hard labor another church stood above the ashes, a little larger than the first to accommodate the growing congregation. But once again, while they slept one night, the incendiarist returned; and this church also was reduced to ashes.

Wails of despair rent the morning air, but with grim determination the sturdy group applied themselves to rebuilding, only to see the new structure suffer the same fate as the previous chapels.

Their enemies across the valley boasted of their success; and, waxing bolder, they raided the mission with bows and arrows and tried to argue Paul and the others out of continuing with their newfound God. But the Christians would not yield, for their strength was in God, and He did not fail them. In Laiagam there now stands an even bigger tabernacle, a witness to the true God and His steadfast worshipers. The power of the false god Timango has waned in that district.

Full of zeal for the Lord, Paul made an excursion into nearby Lai Valley proclaiming the story of redemption. As a result of befriending an old man, he interested the man's whole family in the plan of salvation, as illustrated by the picture roll. They set aside a section of ground at Yakananda for a mission station and began to erect a building.

The neighbors, as usual, opposed the entry of the Seven Days into their midst and expressed their doubts to others. Soon a group gathered, and the leader declared that the mission would not be allowed in their valley.

Paul and his friends quietly continued building. One morning the intransigent neighbor and his group confronted the mission band. While Paul contended that every man has the right to choose his religion, the other side insisted that they did not want the Seven Day mission in their vicinity.

Angered by Paul's defense, the leader of the opposition seized a stick and threatened to beat Paul if he did not leave immediately. When Paul refused, his infuriated opponent struck him, and others joined in with fists, beating him on the face and back until the blood flowed freely. When he fell, they kicked him and jumped on him. Hearing the tumult, the chief came racing to the scene and saved Paul from certain death.

Painfully Paul rose to his feet and faced his enemies. "Me no got cross along you fella," he assured them in the spirit of his divine Master. "Me sorry along you fella tasol, because Timango spoil 'im tink tink belong you. Now we like shake hand along you fella." (I am not cross with you. I am only sorry for you because Timango has spoiled your thinking. Now I want to shake your hands.) While blood dripped from his injuries, Paul went up to his tormentors and shook their hands. The now angry chief threatened to take the offenders to the government post at Wabag for punishment, but Paul interceded.

To settle the argument, the chief asked those who wanted to follow the Seven Day mission to stand behind Paul and the others to line up separately. A large number sided with the champion of the gospel, won by his Christlike spirit under extreme provocation. Thus love triumphed over hate and the church was built.

One of our apostles across the valley from Mulitaka was eighteen-year old Evela, who had received only two years of education in a mission school. Under his ministry a group soon responded to the gospel and some prepared for entrance into the church.

One day a man and his wife decided to take one of their pigs to another village near Evela's outpost. Setting out in the morning with their four-year-old daughter, the father led the pig, while the mother struggled along with a heavy load of kau kau. When they reached their destination several hours later, they were surprised that the daughter was not already with friends in the village. They decided she had been lost along the way.

Accompanied by the villagers, the parents retraced their steps, calling to the little girl as they went. As daylight began to wane, they searched feverishly, for it was not likely that the naked child could survive the night in the open. Using burning sticks for light, the people continued their search in the rain and cold.

Desperate with anxiety, the parents walked back and forth along the trail all night, calling the name of their daughter. Occasionally they made a fire and huddled over it for warmth. Early in the morning they roused the villagers, and once again the area all along the length of the track was diligently searched, but without success. At the end of the day there was still no trace of the missing child.

On the third day, Evela visited this village and found the people preparing a feast for Timango. He was angry and must be appeased so that he would help them in their search. Evela told them that the true God would help them because He loved them. It was not necessary to appease Him. If they would cease their useless preparations for the feast and bow their heads, Evela would pray for them. In simple faith he petitioned God to demonstrate His love and interest in the people by helping them to find the lost child.

Evela then walked through the jungle alone, calling the girl's name. After a short time he heard a faint whimper. He found the child lying under a bush stiff with cold. Without food or a stitch of clothing, she had survived two cold, rainy nights.

Lightheartedly, Evela carried the girl back to the village. With boundless gratitude the tearful parents clasped her in their arms, while the whole village acknowledged the superiority of the true God.

14

Defying Timango

"House 'e fire! House 'e fire!"

I swung around as Paul pointed to flames eagerly crawling up the wall behind me. The fire came from an ingenious chimney of drums, milk tins, bark, and clay that was constructed to convey the smoke through the wall of my new hut. As the dry thatched roof caught, I thought there was no hope of extinguishing the flames, so we hastily threw our patrol equipment out of the door and window.

But dozens of whooping villagers swarmed onto the roof, pulling the thatch apart and beating out the fire, saving most of the walls. It was a sobering experience, which could have occurred while we were sleeping.

The previous morning I had left Wabag by Land Rover with Mr. Cliff Butler, a carpenter from the mission hospital at Sopas. My object was to penetrate Maramun Valley in defiance of Timango who had long reigned. Several national evangelists had already begun there and had reported an encouraging response.

As we climbed up the Lai valley toward Mulitaka, we were suddenly stopped by a twelve-foot gap in the road. A huge boulder crashing down the mountainside on a mad rush to the river below had taken part of the road with it.

An abandoned vehicle nearby intimated that someone had decided to walk rather than attempt to patch the gap. But it would have added more than twenty miles to our hike if we left our conveyance here. So to make a crossing Cliff and I and our helpers collected loose poles and planks from the bridge not far away. An hour later a makeshift bridge looked barely safe, but I decided to risk passing over. Taking off the Land Rover's door for easy exit in case it became necessary to jump out, I hugged the cliff as closely as possible and nervously drove across to the other side without mishap.

"It looks as though Timango does not appreciate our venture," I remarked to Cliff as we drove happily on for the next twenty miles to the end of the road. Two hours later we walked the last half mile into the Mulitaka station and slept in the new grass hut that caught fire the following morning.

After the excitement of the fire had died down, we set out toward Maramun Valley. On our way we passed two growing outstations, whose adherents warmly welcomed us. We climbed steeply through a weird moss forest, where gaunt giants of the jungle fling their dead arms skyward as if imploring help from above. We paused on the 10,000-foot pass for a welcome rest, although the atmosphere was cold, damp, and misty.

Rain began to fall, and we sloshed our way through mud and tripped over tree roots for several hours before halting for the night at an unmanned government rest camp. We were at 9,000 feet in a shallow forested basin rimmed by high mountains.

The mountain men are experts in gathering firewood and making a fire when everything is wet. They cut down into the center of a dead log until they find dry wood to start the fire. In these conditions it is a luxury to peel off one's muddy socks and pour hot water on the aching muscles.

Leaving the eternal mist of these heights, we found the track, which followed a cascading stream four thousand feet down to the isolated Maramun Valley. We slipped and slid continually.

As the morning wore on, I began to feel miserable. My bones and muscles ached; the temperature was rising; the trail became a nightmare. Although my legs became as heavy as rock, I had to keep going. Finally we arrived at the mission outstation. Our lonely believers in this place, never having been visited by their missionary leader before, insisted on shaking hands. But I thought the one hundred handshakes were too much for me. How would I regain strength for the return trek?

During the three days in the valley, we held meetings and dedicated a church. The earnest believers offered special prayers for my recovery, and I improved dramatically. The return trip seemed very long and tiring, but on the second day we eventually trudged through the last few yards of mud and sank into the comfort of the Land Rover. But the excursion had been worth the effort. New outposts had been strengthened and the gospel more firmly established in another of the "uttermost parts."

South of Laiagam is a mountain 12,000 feet high, where storms gather almost daily and send vicious squalls into the Kandep Valley. The floor of this valley is at 7,600 feet altitude. It is graced by several lakes which vary in size according to the season and the amount of rain that falls. About 7,000 tribespeople live here.

Our evangelists had already entered. Anxious to encourage these men, I decided to walk to this valley. With most of the population living on the hills surrounding the flat valley, care for the people is particularly difficult. Their gardens are eight thousand feet or more above sea level. Food grows slowly and sparingly. *Kau kau,* their staple diet, takes nine months to mature. Occasional frosts cause near-famine conditions. Once, when Yamau, a worker from this valley, came to visit me, he looked so gaunt I failed to recognize him. In two months he had lost fifteen pounds, but he spoke nothing of it.

After a refreshing pause on the pass, we slid down the steep mountainside and reached the rest house just as a deluge of rain descended. In the morning we negotiated the hills and squished through a marsh, and shortly after midday we reached Pindak, our main mission station in the valley. Everyone there gave us a sincere welcome.

On this occasion I was honored to dedicate a neat church just fifteen minutes' walk from the uncontrolled area called Wagie. Scores were attending worship services here and indicated a growing love for the Lord. There was promise of large congregations growing up in Pindak and throughout the valley.

Another new outpost we visited was situated on a bleak

mountain ridge, but the people were responsive and enthusi-
astic. Sitting apart was a dejected-looking woman wearing endless strings of beads of mourning called "Job's tears." Upon
being questioned, she said the last of her four children had just
died. Then came her plaintive plea that wrung my heart, "Please
sendim help because me fella die all the same four leg." (Please
send us help, for we die like animals.) The best I could do was
to leave for a few weeks an orderly who was with me.

Returning along the same trail a few days later, I was told
that a chief at Porgeramanda was very anxious for help from
our mission. When we arrived at his village, a pig feast was in
progress, attended with the usual excitement. The people were
so engrossed in their feasting that they did not come forward to
greet us. I waited awhile, glad of the excuse for a rest. Just as
we were about to leave, a man arrived in the village and announced to us, "Me like 'im Seven Day mission." Some of the
other men laughed and mocked at his boldness, but he told me
he had refused any part in the pig feast and would like an
evangelist to settle among his people.

I noticed that the speaker wore two arrow scars on his upper
chest and one on each side, but none on his back. Obviously he
was a veteran warrior who always faced his enemies and could
be depended upon to support staunchly the mission of his
choice. I told him to build a hut and we would try to supply
someone. An evangelist was sent, and this brave man accepted
Christ.

As I saw a plane take off from the government airstrip in the
Kandep Valley and climb into the blue, my heart ached. Aircraft belonging to the various companies and other missions
regularly flew into this valley in a few minutes, while we still
had to labor over the tortuous tracks. Having been a pilot myself for many years, I found this situation particularly galling.
"How long, O God," I lamented, "must we wait for our own
plane?"

Seeing the Land Rover waiting at the end of the vehicular
road next day, we rejoiced. After plodding the muddy trails, we
found bumping along the road on wheels a satisfying experi-

ence. The twelve-mile drive to Laiagam took us one hour and the hike two days. We could have flown the total distance in fifteen minutes.

Flowing through Laiagam is the Lagaip River, which continues northwest to Mulitaka, twelve miles downstream. Two miles farther on the road terminates, and beyond, the gorge deepens and habitation thins till it fades out altogether. A few miles down this gorge at that time was uncontrolled territory, the government not yet having given permission for missionaries to enter. But toward the border were several mission stations which I decided to visit.

Pastor Lionel Smith, an Australian missionary of Irian Barat (formerly known as West New Guinea), accompanied me on this trip. At the first outpost we found a woman whose unbelieving husband, because she wanted to be a Christian, had poured boiling water over her. She recovered in a hospital.

Crossing over a frail swinging bridge made of vines and poles is a creaking, nerve-testing experience. Once on the other side, we followed the river to our last place of call, where the evangelist was building a church.

Beyond this the track led up a huge shale landslide to a high ridge pointing to a gorge hundreds of feet below. In the center of the gorge rose a massive peak with almost sheer walls, marking the boundary of the uncontrolled territory, where hundreds of tribesmen had never heard the name of Jesus. We yearned to proclaim the good news of salvation to them.

The evening meal consisted of *kau kau,* pumpkin, and beans purchased from the villagers and made into a stew. Then we enjoyed biscuits brought from home as we sipped a hot drink. We always carried a portable radio on these patrols for listening to local and overseas news. This particular evening I pricked up my ears as the local news came on. "Listen!" I shouted to Lionel, who was reclining on his cot. "The administrator has just declared that the country west of here is now open, so we can enter there tomorrow."

"Incredible!" said Lionel.

We crossed the boundary early the next day with light hearts.

Excited at being the first to bear the good tidings to this area, after several hours of walking we came upon a group of villagers making a hut. They looked at us with a nonchalant air and kept on working; but they did cast an occasional glance at us.

The children overcame their shyness first and squatted around us chatting like a flock of magpies. With the aid of the picture roll we talked to them, and soon these little ones were singing "Jesus Loves Me," bright eyes beaming with delight. Slowly the men drifted over, then the women, and before long we had a good audience. They were intrigued by the pictures and the news that the God-Man Jesus had defeated Timango. To judge from appearances this fell like music on the ears of some.

But the burly chief rose with a scowl on his face and started to talk. It was obvious that he was unhappy about something. The interpreter told us that he did not want the Seven Day mission among his people because he had heard that they forbade the eating of pig.

Explanations and friendliness availed us nothing, and I commented to Lionel, "Well, it's a long way to come just to be told this."

Then a man of small stature stood up. He also wore a frown, but I noticed he was cleaner and there were no charms hanging from his neck. He said that what the chief had told us was his own decision, but not all the people concurred in it. Pigs, he said, were filthy and the cause of many disputes. He had long since given all of his away. He pleaded with us not to leave the district till we had given someone to instruct the interested people in God's way of life. Ever since visiting an Adventist mission elsewhere, this man had waited for the "clean" mission to come to his village.

Fortunately, we were able to leave an evangelist, and soon a group was following the Lord. But the man who had waited for our coming suffered for stating his convictions. Enemies of the mission came to the station one day and asked who had requested the Seven Days to settle there. When our supporter stepped forward, saying that he had done so, he was seized by two men who held his hands while a third struck him in the face, breaking several of his teeth. But he did not attempt to retaliate. Since then this man has become a member of the church and joyfully looks forward to the coming of Christ.

Thus His work goes on despite difficulties. Lack of men slows us down. Restricted budgets harass us. But "our General, who never makes a mistake, says to us: 'Advance; enter new territory; lift the standard in every land.' . . .

"Our watchword is to be, onward, ever onward. Angels of heaven will go before us to prepare the way. Our burden for the regions beyond can never be laid down till the whole earth is lightened with the glory of the Lord."—*Gospel Workers*, page 470.

15

To Find a Plane

Lying west of Laiagam, remote and almost inaccessible, is a valley renowned for its gold. Mighty bulwarks of jagged rock rise defiantly for thousands of feet, while deep gorges and impenetrable jungle combine to resist the intruder.

Even before government patrols penetrated Porgera, a lone prospector ventured in, undaunted by the rigors of the track. Here, in the turbulent river that gushes from a rocky escarpment, he found gold. After months of toil and hardship he returned to civilization with the precious metal that made him wealthy.

Beautiful in its grandeur and awesome in its ruggedness, this valley still holds fabulous wealth deeply buried beneath masses of rock.

When he returned from his prospecting, the gold miner brought men from the valley to work on his coffee plantation at Goroka. Among these was Emai, a young pigmy five feet tall and puny in build. He wore only a piece of cloth and a bunch of leaves hanging from his waist. But in Emai's heart was a yearning for something more satisfying than the glitter of gold.

One day he was persuaded by a friend to visit an Adventist mission station at Bena Bena, and here he found what he was seeking—peace of mind and joy in his newly found Lord and Saviour. Eventually Emai joined the church, and with unquenchable happiness he returned to his distant village. Here he proclaimed the love of God and the way of salvation with such earnestness that hearts were won.

(74)

When the government opened this rugged area for mission penetration, I led a band of workers in. Mud, mountains, tropical downpours, and the burning sun almost discouraged us, but our efforts were rewarded the first Sabbath. At Tibinin village, where Emai's faithful witness had raised up a group of believers, already four had been baptized. And the villagers showed eagerness to know more about the God of love.

After telling them of the beautiful promise that our Saviour had made to save us from death, and after describing the wonders and glories of heaven, I asked those who wanted to go there to raise their hands. Up went a score of hands, young and old. A group of children, who were sitting in front and had just been taught to sing "Jesus Loves Me," raised their hands.

Following the service, the chief arose and pointed to certain men and women whom he said he would allow to go to heaven. But he would not permit a little girl sitting in front to go. She excitedly protested, big tears streaming down her grimy face, saying no one would stop her from going to heaven. With some effort I managed to pacify her. Then I told the chief that God was preparing homes for *everyone* who loved and obeyed Him.

At Bopen village also, Emai had planted precious seeds, and many desired to unite with the body of Christ. Chiefs came in from other villages and pleaded for spiritual help. They had seen the radiant happiness of Emai.

The next day was mercilessly hot, the sun beating down on our backs as we toiled up a steep mountainside. After two hours we reached the summit and lay down exhausted under a large tree, refreshed by a cooling breeze. In the distance we saw a Cessna aircraft land on a little airstrip carved out of mud and mountain. After an interval it took off with a burst of power, climbed, and disappeared toward the north. Again I questioned why the Adventist mission did not have a plane.

For three days we had been toiling over mountains and through mud. It would take us four more tiresome hours to hike to the airstrip. Planes could fly from there to Laiagam in fifteen minutes. How long would it be before we could speed up God's work by flying over the obstacles that delayed us on the ground? Eighteen years had passed since I took my training as a pilot, but I had to be patient yet a little longer.

About midday we came across three men and four boys who were laboriously carrying soil from a cliff to a sluice box. Happy for an excuse to rest, we watched as they huddled intently over the sluice, washing the soil away with running water and looking for the glint of gold. The leader asked me whether I would like to see what he had found that morning. From a dirty bag hanging over his shoulder he took a small tin that he opened. Within were seven flakes of gold averaging about one grain each.

So much work for so little gain, I thought. But as I expressed my astonishment, the miner told me that even a little gold is of considerable value; so the toil and sweat were worthwhile to him. I compared the miner who first discovered gold here with Emai. Though Emai received no gold, he worked with even greater zeal and joyfully endured suffering. Instead of a shovel and a goldpan, he carried a picture roll and a simple gramophone. He had indeed found the true gold, the pure gold of Porgera that was considered of highest value in heaven. In the sight of men Emai is only a pygmy, but in the eyes of God he is of great stature.

During a mission workers' meeting at Laiagam I was shyly approached by Ruap, who intimated that he wished to be married. The prospective bride was a mission girl and would make a good wife for an evangelist. So the ceremony was performed in the church a few days later, wedding a couple not far removed from heathenism who had asked God's benediction upon their marriage in His house. The heathen purchase brides with pigs and shells, the woman becoming little more to her husband than a degraded chattel, living with the pigs in a filthy hut.

For Ruap and his young wife the future would be very different. They expressed the desire that burned within them to share the faith that had so completely changed their lives. They were first appointed to a place Ruap had already visited. The journey took them over a 10,000-foot pass, where one misstep would mean dropping to death hundreds of feet below. But there was beauty in the torrents that tumbled down the mountain and in the gorgeous birds of paradise which flew across the track.

After several days the couple emerged from a rain forest into a clearing and were joyously greeted by Ruap's heathen friends. Slowly a simple mission station arose, first a dwelling hut and then a church.

Then a morning came when Ruap's mind was restless and his body hot. When night came he slept poorly, and the next day his aching body made every movement painful. The simple medicines he had brought gave him no relief.

The following day Ruap found to his dismay that his legs could not support him; so he appealed to some of the village men to make a stretcher and carry him to medical aid. They protested that the track was too steep and dangerous, but Ruap insisted that he must get help. Bowing his head, he asked God to care for the work he must leave behind and to help the carriers convey him safely over the terrible trail.

The near-naked savages started along the narrow path, and the young wife tearfully followed. For long hours with Ruap lashed to the stretcher, they struggled and stumbled on the steeply rising and falling track.

At last the walking ambulance reached the medical aid post recently established by the government. Here they stayed for several hours, while the orderly gave Ruap injections. But these failed to help him, and his legs became completely paralyzed.

Reluctantly the men decided to carry the patient to a hospital on the other side of a high pass. Knowing this track, I marvel that he was transported over it. Steep grades and precipitous gorges make it a nightmare even when walking empty-handed. Rain, cold, and the danger of slipping added to the hazards. But they went on hour after hour.

Finally the sad little band arrived at Laiagam, and word was sent to me at Wabag. I requested the government to arrange an aircraft to bring Ruap to Wabag, which they did. But for unavoidable reasons the plane was delayed two days, and finally the patient was transported by Land Rover. Weak and wasted, he arrived at the mission hospital. For eight long days Ruap had suffered intensely, while life ebbed out of his legs and well-nigh out of his whole body. The doctor repeatedly exclaimed, "if only he had come sooner!"

Although both his legs were paralyzed, I always found Ruap smiling, and never did he complain or question God's dealings with him. He would grasp his legs, demonstrating that they could be moved only by his hands. It took several weeks to convince Ruap of the awful truth that never again would his feet tramp the mountains with the gospel of peace. Under sympathetic medical treatment his condition improved, but the disease had relentlessly taken its toll. However, Ruap was delighted when, in spite of his serious disability, he could care for a small company of worshipers.

My valiant band of workers had struggled against great odds to bring the glad tidings of great joy to distant areas. And our lines were growing perilously long and thin. Budgets were lean, evangelists scarce. Logic demanded that we halt our expansion, but to do so would be to ignore the providences of God's forward leading.

While our men toiled painfully over the mountains, missionaries of other denominations and their personnel flew comfortably overhead. Could our evangelists, with their wives and families, be expected to continue this way? Why couldn't we have a plane?

A faithful worker and his wife were descending the mountain to Porgera, with their baby son carried in a *biloom* hanging from the mother's head. She slipped, and the infant's spine struck the root of a tree. He was in the hospital several weeks recovering from the painful injury that threatened to cause paralysis. Surely we were expecting too much of our workers and their wives.

In the near future the government planned to open to missionaries a particularly remote area called Lake Kopiago. Traveling there by foot, over extremely difficult terrain, took eleven days. How could we do it?

To me there was one obvious answer. Again I pleaded with

God to provide an aircraft. The evangelists also offered special prayers on this theme. The government had already built airstrips in most of the remote valleys. A plane would reduce days of hardship to minutes of comfortable travel.

Before I left for furlough at the end of the year, money mysteriously began to flow in toward this specific project. All who knew me were aware that for nearly twenty years I had hoped to introduce a plane into mission service. The greeting of some of my friends had become, "Well, Len, when is your mission plane coming?"

"Tomorrow!" was my standard reply.

At this time I inquired from our newly elected union president, Pastor O. D. F. McCutcheon, whether a gift plane would be accepted. He replied that very likely it would be gladly accepted. The same day a committee was convened and action was taken that, subject to the approval of the Australasian Division, should a plane be offered to the union mission as a gift, it would be accepted. It appeared that the Lord was leading in the direction I had hoped for so long.

The subject of planes for mission use had long been debated throughout the world field. General Conference action had been taken authorizing use of aircraft under certain conditions, stipulating safe standards for pilot and passengers.

The use of commercial aircraft for our field work had been tried, but where operations were some distance from the base of air companies, as my district work was, the cost was prohibitive. I once chartered a plane from the nearest base, at Mount Hagen, to fly me from Wabag to Porgera and to pick me up again five days later. The cost was $165.60, whereas operating a mission aircraft from my base at Laiagam I could fly to Porgera and return in thirty minutes for $7.50. When the missionary himself is also the pilot, the plane waits for him; and when his duties are finished, he can leave immediately.

We awaited further developments with growing expectation.

16

A Plane at Last

Gazing for the first time upon a crashed war plane in the jungle of New Guinea in 1942, I was filled with conflicting emotions. I was amazed at the complexity of the machine, now a crumpled mass of metal with electronic gadgets, wires, pipes, dials, and controls scattered around—complex and costly, but for the purpose of destruction.

Many a night the drone of enemy engines aroused me from sleep in the jungle; and, fascinated, I arose to watch the long fingers of the searchlights raking the sky to find the marauders, and to listen to the thunder of the ack-ack guns as they splashed daubs of red in the dark sky. But the fascination waned suddenly when later I heard the swish of falling enemy bombs.

Soon the Allied forces grew, and I witnessed mighty armadas of bombers and fighters roaring off Seven Mile airstrip behind Port Moresby and again at Dobadura, as pulverizing raids were launched against Rabaul and other enemy strongholds.

All this huge expenditure of men and matériel was so often used to bring death and destruction. But when the war was over, would there not be a great potential here for good? Thus began in me an unquenchable yearning to fly over these jungles on missions of mercy and goodwill.

After four years in the army in New Guinea I was discharged and returned to my homeland, New Zealand, for a few months. Here I joined an aero club and met Mr. Brian Haybittle, a World War I pilot, who taught me to fly.

I do not think Brian was overawed by my progress, but those

were days of keen excitement for me. The Tiger Moth, with its open cockpit, gave one the exhilaration of flying, but when exposed to the icy atmosphere at 9,000 feet over snow-clad Mount Egmont in wintertime, I did not find it so pleasant.

We had done several "circuits and bumps" together on one particular day, when Brian got out of the front cockpit and unfastened the forward control stick. Brian shouted above the noise of the idling engine, "Righto, Len, it's all yours now! Take it away and do a few circuits and bumps."

I was on my own, challenging the sky, a moment of great elation. I felt the jolting of the wheels on the turf, then its smooth cessation as the machine mounted into the air. The propeller struggled for speed and height while the engine roared like some living monster throatily voicing its exuberance.

I clearly remember the cold glow of the winter sun setting over the sea and the icy air that bit into my helmeted face. After a few circuits I waddled the aircraft over to the hangar, and when my sister-in-law congratulated me, my frozen face would not permit even a smile in my moment of triumph.

My primary purpose in flying was to be a missionary pilot. However, the Lord was to lead me by a long and devious route before my hope was realized. During the frustrating years of waiting I flew whenever I could, especially on furloughs.

An amazing series of events culminated in the purchase of the first aircraft used by Adventist missionaries in Australasia. During a period of five years only about $1,000 had been contributed to the scheme. Then during the last few months prior to the purchase, $15,000 came in, spontaneously given by many people in different countries.

An elderly lady in the United States caught the vision of our need for a mission plane and gave liberally of her means for the project, working incessantly at various occupations and giving her entire wages to the fund, saying she was determined to see the undertaking through even if it were her last work on earth. A good friend in Hong Kong gave a substantial donation. And in Australia strangers assisted liberally.

In America Dr. Glenn G. Reynolds of Washington, D.C., had

very kindly undertaken to promote the scheme. Halfway through my furlough in 1964 the fund had grown to $12,000, which naturally delighted me. We could now obtain a good used aircraft, so I requested the doctor to set the wheels in motion for the purchase of a Cessna 180.

At this time I visited a former college friend in New Zealand. After exchanging greetings we sat down to enjoy the evening meal together. Then my host startled me by asking, "Well, Len, how much do you need to buy a mission plane?"

"I guess $4,000 would mean the difference between a new and a used plane," I replied.

"There shouldn't be any problem about that," my friend rejoined. "Between my dad, myself, and a friend, I think you can count on it."

I was stunned by this assurance and wired Dr. Reynolds to consider purchasing a new aircraft. By return mail I received a letter telling me that a new plane, fully instrumented, would cost $16,408.75. With the extra donation he would have on hand $16,400, or all but $8.75! Glenn added on the bottom of his letter, "Praise God from whom all blessings flow."

While attending to formalities for the importation and registration of the plane, I requested the Department of Civil Aviation in Australia for the registration letters VH-SDA. Having been informed by an aircraft agency that such an application could not be granted by the department, I was agreeably surprised when it was granted without question.

In Australia all aircraft registrations consist of five letters, the first two always being the country's designation—VH. This is followed by a hyphen and a combination of three letters. Any combination may be used so long as it is not already registered. Thus wherever VH-SDA should fly it would be recognized as the Seventh-day Adventist mission plane.

Unfortunately, I had to return to the mission field before the aircraft arrived in Sydney by boat. Nevertheless I went north with a light heart.

Originally my headquarters was to be established at Mulitaka, twelve miles from Laiagam, the nearest airstrip. Preliminary attempts had been made to lease the ground where Paul Piari had established his first mission station, an ideal central location, and only a few hundred yards from the airstrip. But negotiations had broken down and agreement seemed impossible. However, to our amazement, the attitude of the owners changed, and the transaction was finalized. Living so close to the airstrip was a wonderful convenience when our mission plane arrived.

The Laiagam airstrip had earned a notorious reputation. The strip itself was built on soft white clay. High rainfall encouraged the growth of jellylike algae on its surface, and regular cross winds with severe turbulence complicated the approach.

The assistant district commissioner at Laiagam, Mr. Denys Faithful, also a pilot, decided to improve the airstrip. He surfaced a narrow section down the center with crushed white stone, thus eliminating the surface problem. This was almost completed when our plane arrived. Now a reasonable load could be lifted off the strip regardless of the amount of rain, making it economical for me to operate from Laiagam.

For more than a year we expected the government to open the Lake Kopiago area to missionaries. An airstrip had already been built. This place required an eleven-day trek over difficult terrain, but only thirty-five minutes by air. It opened one month after the plane arrived, allowing me time to familiarize myself with tropical highland conditions and airstrips.

Having been shipped in crates from the United States of America, our plane was assembled and painted in Sydney. I was invited to attend the dedication service for the aircraft and fly with it to New Guinea.

The day dawned bright and fair on June 27, when the *Andrew Stewart* was dedicated and commissioned as the first Adventist mission plane in the South Seas. Appropriately it was named after A. G. Stewart, who commenced mission service in 1903. White-haired but still as upright as a soldier, this eighty-two-year-old stalwart offered the dedicatory prayer. Also participating in the ceremony were missionary veterans W. N. Lock and A. J. Campbell.

Two days later, ferry-pilot Brian Walker and I flew off toward New Guinea, 2,500 miles away. Late in the afternoon of the first day we were well up the tropical coast of Australia when a severe storm near Cairns forced us to return to Townsville. Night was closing in, and the weather was chasing us as we flew on the radio compass and finally touched down on the lighted airport.

The following morning we reached Cairns and continued up featureless Cape York. Tropical haze and drizzle reduced visibility as we left the tip of Australia and flew over Torres Strait. Peering through the murk we saw Thursday Island looming ahead; we landed for fuel and customs formalities.

Majestic storms were scattered along the dreary coast of the Papuan Gulf as we approached, and the mighty Fly River, thirty-five miles wide at its mouth, was emptying the water and soil it had brought down from the shrouded hinterland. We were now only six degrees from the equator. Below stretched miles upon miles of monotonous jungle inhabited by crocodiles and mosquitoes. Because of the unfavorable weather, and having ample fuel, we decided to make our next landing at Goroka, in the New Guinea highlands.

Climbing to nine thousand feet, we managed to keep clear of clouds near the coast; but as the mountains guarding the highlands reached up to meet us, so did the clouds. Mammoth cumulus cloud buildups challenged our advance, so we climbed higher, but in our small plane we could never hope to top the hats of these giants of the heavens.

Ten, eleven, twelve, then thirteen thousand feet registered on the altimeter. Could we find a gap in the clouds? Brian was sitting on the edge of his seat peering ahead, when at fourteen thousand feet a pathway appeared. We flew into it and could see Mount Erimbari, west of Goroka. We both relaxed and enjoyed the downhill run into the valley, soon landing with a feeling of accomplishment.

Pastor McCutcheon was there to meet us with a customary warmhearted greeting. It was grand to be in New Guinea with our first mission aircraft.

17

Boroko

A missionary pilot's life is made up of multitudinous duties. He may fly several hundred hours a year in his local field and other mission areas. He nurtures his churches, whether they be accessible by foot, Land Rover, or plane. He holds regular workers' meetings to keep his band of nationals keen and happy in their service. Then there is the pastoral care and, of course, office work.

As I sat in my office one morning, I heard a timid knock. Responding to my invitation, in walked Boroko, who lived in a nearby Adventist village. Not knowing a word of pidgin English, he could only smile at me and talk in his own language. I smiled back and talked in pidgin. Then he fumbled in the pocket of his shorts and produced a small tin which he opened ceremoniously. Out of it, Boroko took $6.50, which he handed to me. It was always a delight to see Boroko, for he had a happy disposition and a good sense of humor, although he was a shy soul.

"What name something? Tithe?" I queried. Understanding the last word at least, he nodded with his usual smile. Every two or three weeks he came with his tithe, always insisting that he see me. Each time he was given a receipt, which he carefully folded and placed in his little tithe tin.

I doubted whether such a large amount could be tithe, so I asked a schoolboy to come and question Boroko in his own dialect. It seemed hardly possible that he earned an income ten times greater than the amount he had handed me. Still smiling,

Boroko insisted that it was indeed tithe, and that he wanted to give it to the mission. When I again expressed doubt that the money was tithe only, my visitor was a little hurt, and explained that it was tithe from a sale of firewood. Obviously he wanted to give the money, but I could not help wondering whether he had not given nine tenths and kept one tenth for himself. Whatever proportion it was of his income, he clearly loved giving it to the Lord, and who was I to question him?

But Boroko had a problem. Each time we examined candidates for baptism, he would be right up in the front seat of the church, hoping to be included in the group. But time after time he was passed by. The difficulty was that if he were baptized he could keep only one of his four wives. Boroko himself, after deciding to live with only one wife, found that another one refused to leave him. He wanted only one wife, but he had two. In such cases arrangements are usually made with the clan of the departing wife for her to remarry or otherwise to be provided for.

Eventually the problem was solved and the greatest event in Boroko's life took place—he was baptized, in the name of the Father, the Son, and the Holy Spirit. His joy knew no bounds, and for days thereafter he could be seen visiting his friends and telling them of his gladness. His faithfulness in tithe paying continued, and his perpetual smile was broader than ever.

One day Boroko went down to the nearby stream to do his washing. The spot where he waded in with his precious clothing and a small piece of soap, was narrow, steep, and slippery. He soaped, rubbed, and rinsed his garments, humming one of the many gospel choruses he had learned. When he had finished, he tossed his clothes up the bank onto a clump of grass; then, still humming, he thoroughly lathered himself.

All this time Boroko had been completely oblivious of the fact that he was slowly edging toward deep water. Suddenly he slipped down the steep slope of the shelf where he had been standing and fell beneath the surface. A man of the mountains, he had never learned to swim. Completely submerged, he started to stumble along the bottom of the stream.

Then, realizing his situation was critical, Boroko quickly prayed, "Lord, I am paying my tithe faithfully, I am living with only one wife, and now I am baptized. You know how much I love You. Now I want You to save me." No sooner had his thoughts ascended to his heavenly Father than he felt something scrape his head. He reached up and grasped it. It was a branch from an overhanging tree, which he used to pull himself to safety.

Now doubly full of the joy of the Lord, Boroko decided to make a visit to relatives in a distant part of the jungle to pass on the good news. Hour after hour he trudged through the fetid forest, ignoring the slush, stinging nettles, and leeches. Late in the afternoon he arrived at his destination, wet and muddy, grateful to be able to sit on the dirt floor of his relatives' hut to dry before the cheery fire. He satisfied his hunger with *kau kau* cooked in the hot coals and slept peacefully.

For the next few days Boroko spoke of God's love, telling his relatives of his own conversion and his being spared from drowning. Many responded. On his return home Boroko, with glowing eyes, came to see me. Joyfully he told of his witnessing, requesting a picture roll, a gramophone, and a few nails to help build a church.

Now in the village of Boroko's relatives stands a little chapel, where many villagers are preparing for baptism, and where each day melodies of praise ascend to God, a witness to the zeal and love of one humble disciple.

As far as practical, I tried to spend each Sabbath at a different mission station. Sharing the triumphs and trials of the believers, walking slippery trails with them, and eating in their humble huts—all this binds us together.

In worship they never fail to respond to a talk on the advent hope. The prospect of living with their beloved Saviour in heaven is their highest delight.

18

Andrew Stewart -- A Missionary Again

It was time for a series of meetings thoughout my area. These were planned well ahead, since both subsidized workers and other members who would attend often had to walk long distances over mountains and through valleys, carrying sufficient food for the duration of the meetings and the return trip.

These difficulties did not deter the people from coming. They love the services and the pictures projected on the screen. And the periods between meetings become social occasions which brighten the drab New Guinea life.

After loading the aircraft with Dorcas clothing, soap, camping gear, etcetera, Paul and I climbed aboard the *Andrew Stewart*. Laiagam Valley showed patches of sunlight, but the mountaintops that flanked the valley pierced the clouds that settled above them. Taking off, we circled for height in the valley and then headed toward Porgera Valley, where we knew hundreds would be waiting for the special weekend meetings.

It soon became evident, however, that not only were the ridgetops and peaks covered with mist, but clouds poured through Porgera Valley Pass, obliterating all treetops and flowing downward along the treacherous air currents. Not a glimpse of the valley could be seen. No hope from this direction.

"Me no enough along find 'im road along this fella half [I am unable to find an entrance this way]," I said to Paul. Although normally a man of boundless courage, Paul rarely enjoyed flying and readily agreed to try another route.

Farther down the Laiagam Valley was another approach to

the Porgera Valley, known as the bad weather route, where the pass was only 7,000 feet high. We headed there. The jagged peak jutting up from the floor of the narrow valley in the vicinity of this pass made it easy to locate.

Circling near this prominent landmark, I saw that there was no place below for a forced landing. I was grateful that our dependable Continental engine kept purring without missing a beat. It was soon obvious that clouds had settled into this pass also, barring passage. As I continued to circle I prayed that the Lord would open the way so I could meet the waiting people.

As we gained altitude near the pass, we discovered a distinct pathway through the clouds and followed it. Once over the pass, glimpses of the valley below allowed me to fix my position every minute or so. Now the important question was whether or not the airstrip was open. Being at the high end of the valley, it was probably shrouded in the mist or obliterated by rain. But we flew trustingly on, the sky still being clear at our level. Finally, almost over the strip, we were looking for it intently. If we could not land in two minutes we would have to turn back.

Paul saw it first. "Place balus 'e stop!" he shouted. And there it was beneath us, with neither rain nor mist to frighten us away. I sighed with relief and thanked the Master Pilot.

"Me please too much along lookim face belong you," chorused the waiting workers. Only a short time before, they told me, a plane had circled overhead and returned. No sooner had we taken our goods to our mission station near the strip than clouds closed in and rain poured down.

We are told of the One "who maketh the clouds His chariot; who walketh upon the wings of the wind." "His strength is in the clouds," with "snow, and vapors; stormy winds fulfilling His word." Time and again, while flying for the Lord, I have found a pathway through the clouds leading me where duty called.

Some time later our second mission aircraft was ferried from the United States to New Guinea via the Pacific by two gallant pilots, Wayne and Darrel Fowler. While it was being modified at Goroka, I took Wayne to Laiagam in VH-SDA so that he could see firsthand the value of aircraft in our mission program.

As we approached Wabag and continued into Laiagam, mighty tropical storms lashed the mountains and swooped into the valleys; but by skirting around these we were easily able to reach our destination. But ahead, toward Porgera, a gigantic storm completely obliterated the mountains and valleys. We could see only ominous clouds above and dark water beneath.

On landing at Wabag I learned from a missionary friend of another organization—we had received the message through their own radio hookup—that one of our workers was critically ill at Porgera. It was necessary to pick him up and take him to a hospital; but in spite of the urgency of the case, prudence dictated that we wait until the savage storm had spent its fury.

Two hours later, at five o'clock, we took off to assess the weather. Toward Porgera the heavy precipitation had ended, leaving only several storm cells which were moving westward. There were still patches of rain, but these could be avoided.

We flew between clumps of cloud toward the high end of the valley, intermittently catching sight of the mountains below. This allowed me to pinpoint our position. Nearby Mount Mc-Nicholl reared its craggy head 12,000 feet upwards, so we climbed to 13,000 feet, and saw the sodden summit between clouds. Three minutes later we were flying over the head of Porgera Valley. Circling masses of cloud, we suddenly saw a gap stretching right down to the valley. Cautiously we descended, leaving over our shoulder a way of retreat.

Water was cascading down the sides of the strip, and every stream was a torrent. We found ourselves in a large pocket of clear air centered over the strip. Down the valley about five hundred yards from the runway a vertical wall of mist rose right from the ground till it lost itself in the storm clouds above. It looked as though a huge hand had swept the mist and clouds away from the landing area and piled them into a huge heap.

Our workers were exuberant when they saw us land. Hope had vanished when they saw the big storm invade the valley. We loaded the sick man aboard, shook hands with our faithful band, offered prayer, and flew away. Within an hour the patient was under skillful medical care at Sopas Hospital.

Despite early problems, mission work in Porgera Valley progressed steadily. When the evangelists first went there, they found a serious shortage of food caused by the slow rate of growth in such a high valley. To procure what was needed, the leader several times had to walk half a day down the valley to a lower altitude and carry food back. Besides this, the first leader, Kaipe, lost his home and few valuable belongings when his hut was accidentally burned.

The mission thus established in sacrifice was now bearing choice fruit. Since my early walkabout, five new stations had begun to operate, and more recently I had dedicated three new churches.

One of the first converts was a leper who had been treated at the Wabag government hospital. While there he consistently attended church at an Adventist mission. Upon returning home, this exuberant man won his wife and daughter for the Lord.

His feet were crippled by the ravages of the disease; nevertheless, with the assistance of other villagers, he built a hut and planted a garden. Then he insisted that we give him an evangelist. This we were able to do, and a company of believers was begun in this man's village.

Once when on a visit to this valley, I opened the door of my hut and saw several wild men talking excitedly to Paul. Their eyes flashed as they clutched their bows and arrows. I learned that they were talking about a young girl whom we had named Lily because of her relatively light skin. They were related to her and strongly opposed her wish to be baptized. They said they had arranged for her to be married to a heathen man who was in the process of paying the bride price, several large pigs.

I told these men that the decision to be baptized was a personal one, and no person had the right to forbid another to take the step. Further, Lily had been examined and found ready to receive this rite, which was to be performed that day. This angered the men even more. One suggested that if we paid them they would withdraw their protests. I informed them that this proposition could not be considered. Their last word, as they strode away, was a threat that Lily would be killed if she went ahead with her plans. I knew this was not an idle threat, as only recently a girl belonging to another mission in this same valley had been killed after her baptism.

While we were talking, Lily was standing shyly in the background. She heard every word spoken and understood the truculent attitude of her relatives. Calling her over, I emphasized the peril she faced and assured her I would understand if she wished to defer her baptism. The decision rested with her.

Without hesitation, Lily looked up and quietly answered, "Me like baptize today. Me ready finish along die." My heart was deeply stirred by Lily's earnestness and determination.

After a refreshing service of rededication in the church, the crowd of several hundred started down to the nearby stream to see the eighteen candidates publicly witness to their acceptance of Christ. Lily was one of the white-robed group. Her relatives, still carrying bows and arrows, followed in the rear. A subdued expression of happiness on her face reflected both her joy and her apprehension. Her decision made, she would not turn back.

At the water's edge I reminded the onlookers and candidates of the significance of baptism and urged those who were not church members to follow the example of the group who were now to receive the sacred rite. Lily's relatives, faces giving no indication of inner feelings, squatted on a boulder overlooking the scene. "Lord," I prayed, "touch their hearts."

Then the candidates stepped into the water, and I began baptizing them. My back was turned toward her enemies as Lily's turn came. Without even casting a glance in their direction, she stepped forward, calm and serene. I immersed her in the name of the Trinity, and I added a special entreaty that she be strengthened in her resolution and that the hearts of those who planned to kill her should be softened.

Although Lily could not safely move far from the mission station after this, she was protected from the threatened evil, and today she is married to a dedicated evangelist. Together God is using them to subdue cruel hearts. Even Lily's relatives are reconciled to her religion; and I hope that someday, because of her courageous stand, they also will be converted.

19

The Accident

The chief surgeon's face was grim as he examined my lacerated leg. Nurses standing by drew sharp breaths. And three assisting doctors looked at each other and slowly shook their heads. Undoubtedly the leg must be amputated.

In this desperate situation I had prayed aloud, "O Lord, thank You for saving my life. Now give me words to persuade the doctors not to amputate. You can heal my leg—I know You can."

Now, still conscious despite the rising flood of pain, I looked into the set faces of the medical staff. They could see the pleading in my eyes. "Please save my leg," I implored. "I am a Christian missionary, pilot of the plane. God will heal my leg if you apply your skill. Many people will be praying for me. Please—" My voice trailed off. What more could I say?

I saw by the doctors' hasty consultations and guarded expressions that they held little hope of being able to accede to my request. The damage was too extensive. "There is no chance," a spokesman said.

I looked at my wife's distressed face. A needle was inserted into a vein, and I floated off into painless oblivion.

Only thirty minutes earlier I had walked across the runway to the mission aircraft as it stood on the wide Mount Hagen airstrip. It was a beautiful morning, and life was good. Light mists were dissipating from the purple velvet of New Guinea's central mountain ranges, and the mile-high Wahgi Valley was a fertile patchwork of coffee and tea plantations and tiny gardens. This was the time to fly, before the mighty tropical storms built up on the 15,000-foot ranges and drifted across the valley.

Today I would escape the tedium of office work, flying for God. I intended to visit several mission stations, transferring national workers, taking missionaries to remote airstrips for patrols, and transporting students to their home districts after the college year. It would take perhaps two days, and I was ready.

After warming up the engine for a minute or so, I opened up the throttle and taxied across the runway to the spot where my passengers and cargo were waiting. For my first flight there were a national teacher and his wife for Kainantu, two friends for Goroka, and another for Madang on the coast. Shutting down the engine by pulling the lean mixture control out, I waited till the engine stopped and then turned the ignition key off. Climbing out, I filed my flight plan with the airport control tower.

At the front of the plane I began a further routine inspection before flying. I tested the propeller spinner for looseness and checked the edge of the eighty-eight-inch blades for bad nicks and cracks. To test for compression I reached high and grasped the tip of the propeller with my right hand and pulled down. There was good compression in that cylinder. But there are six cylinders. So I raised my right hand again and, unconsciously, my left leg. Then suddenly, by a remote chance, the engine fired and the propeller spun.

Mercifully, the following second was a blank. The next thing I remember was finding myself lying on the runway ten feet from the plane, my left leg almost severed above the knee. Although I had been hurled ten feet, my injured leg lay in front of me as though carefully placed there by unseen hands.

Then things moved rapidly. I grabbed the gory stump to arrest the bleeding. My distracted wife rushed over to me. "Help! Help!" she shouted as she too held the stump tightly. One of the passengers ran over to the control tower and another to the terminal and raised the alarm. The airpost ambulance raced across, and its crew fastened a tourniquet around my leg. Then followed the seven bumpy miles to town and the hospital.

As the fight for my leg began, I could not keep quiet. I knew the bone was severely shattered and the flesh cut so deeply that only a flap of skin and muscle connected the lower leg.

Since there was no blood bank in this remote part of New Guinea, a nurse at the hospital nobly gave hers. Before leaving the operating room my wife asked, "Isn't there something you can do to save the leg?"

"No, I'm afraid not," replied the doctor.

During the operation one of the doctors went out to the waiting room and said to my wife, "I'm so sorry we have to amputate the leg."

A friend phoned the hospital, and my wife answered to his query, "Yes, they have amputated it."

But the struggle was not over. More and more knees were bent as the news spread. All pleaded with God to overrule. The skillful surgeon, who had been a heart surgeon in Europe, was steadily working, assessing the damage, struggling against the obvious decision to amputate, wanting to save the leg. I am sure angels hovered in the operating room also.

As soon as our division office in Sydney received the news, President L. C. Naden called the brethren together for special prayer. Throughout the churches in the homeland and from mountain to mountain and valley to valley in New Guinea the news spread, and our believers earnestly implored the Lord on my behalf.

For my wife time dragged on slowly as she kept silent vigil outside the operating room. She picked up one of my shoes. "I must not forget the other one," she thought. Then the stunning truth struck—"He will need only one shoe in the future."

One hour, two hours, and more. Then there was a stir at the operating-room door. I was wheeled out. To my wife's joyous amazement my leg had not been amputated!

"We will try it for three days," said the surgeon. "If it becomes gangrenous, we can remove it at leisure."

Shortly after being placed in the ward I regained consciousness. My mind was clear, and instantly my thought was, "What have they done to my leg?" I raised my right foot beneath the sheet to feel if the other foot was there. Yes! I could feel it, warm and able to move. Joy of joy! "Now God will be able to heal it," I thought. And I did not doubt that He would.

As I lay in bed I pondered. Why did the engine fire if the ignition key was turned off? This was undoubtedly due to the fact that I had warmed the engine up and had run it across the runway, a process which heated carbon in one or more cylinders. As the fuel and air mixture was drawn into the cylinder, this hot carbon had ignited it, causing the engine to fire.

The fact that I had raised my left leg a little only a split second before the propeller started turning brought it within the orbit of the propeller tips. The first blade gashed into my leg just above the kneecap, not too deeply, but its pitch pulled the leg farther into the orbit. The second blade, closer, then cut seriously into the limb six inches higher.

The accident could not have happened at a more inconvenient time, when three of the six Australian missionaries from my corner of the field and the other mission pilot were home on furlough. I was carrying on as before while helping the many hundreds of nationals preparing for baptism.

But how different the outcome of the accident would have been if it had occurred at an airstrip where no appropriate medical aid was available. I regularly fly into extremely remote areas and spend several days there fostering mission interests. In some of these valleys there is no one capable of operating a radio to call emergency help. Thus, with no immediate aid available, the accident would most certainly have proved fatal.

The high degree of efficiency of the departments of civil aviation and public health during this emergency was highly commendable. Within three minutes the airport ambulance had rushed to my rescue. Fifteen minutes later found me on the operating table under the expert care of four doctors and six nurses whose efficiency left nothing to be desired, having even immediate anesthesia ready for injection. For such service in a primitive land like New Guinea I am extremely grateful.

Above all, I praise the Lord for His deliverance and the saving of my leg.

Many years ago I placed at the back of my Bible some thoughtful words by John Ruskin, thinking that someday I might need them. How true they are, and what a comfort they have been to me.

"There is no music in a rest, but there is the making of music in it. In our whole life melody the music is broken off here and there by 'rests,' and we foolishly think we have come to the end of the tune. God sends a time of forced leisure—sickness, disappointed plans, frustrated efforts—and makes a sudden pause in the choral hymn of our lives. . . .

"Not without design does God write the music of our lives. But be it ours to learn the time and not be dismayed at the 'rests.' . . . If we look up, God Himself will beat the time for us. With the eye on Him we shall strike the next note full and clear."

20

Men to Match My Mountains

"Tell me, doctor, why weren't the sciatic nerve and femoral artery severed by the propeller, on the fateful morning of the accident?"

Having returned to New Guinea, I had been anxious to meet again and put this question to Dr. Pavel Kolisch, the talented surgeon specialist who had sewed my almost severed leg together after its encounter with the aircraft propeller. As I had amputated more than one leg myself during my army and post-war medical career, I knew that since the slash was cut more deeply into the leg than the level of these major vessels, they should have been severed. I was intrigued.

"Well," the doctor thoughtfully replied, "the bone was not cut but shattered, and the four-inch chip shown in the X-ray film must have been pushed downward so that it protected the important nerve; and although the artery was badly lacerated, the chip saved it from being completely severed."

"How astonishing," I exclaimed, "and a simple explanation that seems perfectly reasonable." But within me welled up a deeper feeling of wonder and gratitude.

After flying into the Mount Hagen airport for the first time following my recuperation, I was walking to the control tower to submit a flight plan when I was accosted by a company pilot. His parents had been nearby and were early on the scene to see the gash after the accident. He had arrived shortly afterward.

"Did you fly here yourself?" he asked with obvious incredulity.

"I certainly did."

"Well!" he exclaimed. "Now I believe in God! You are one person I thought would never fly again."

Late one afternoon when I was winging my way homeward between storm clouds over the Wabag Valley, the radio came to life: "Sierra Delta Alpha, this is Mike Foxtrot India, see you on 118.1 kilocycles."

I switched on the VHF radio.

"Is that you, Len?" a friendly voice queried.

"Yes, it surely is, and it's grand to be back flying again," I replied.

"Praise the Lord," said the Mission Aviation Fellowship pilot.

"Praise the Lord indeed," I said.

First, I returned to New Quinea for three months, using a walking stick in case I stumbled. The orthopedic surgeon, Mr. Brian Hammond, under whose care I had been in Sydney, informed me that the bone was not very strong yet but prudent use of the leg would help it. Having no problem whatsoever in flying, I was thus able to visit my national workers in the field to encourage and help them. Their solicitude for my recovery and the warmth of their welcome was a touching experience.

I returned to Australia after this trial period, and the doctor assured me the bone was greatly strengthened. Thus it was my pleasure to present him with my New Guinea carved walking stick depicting a crocodile about to grab a dog.

I exult in my work again in the land and among the people I love. No longer can I share their toil and tears on the mountain trails, but I can fly in and out of the valleys to visit them. Most centers are locally headquartered near the airstrips; and, as long as the ground is not slippery or rough, since I am still able to walk several miles, I can carry on my work almost as formerly.

More than twenty years have passed since I took up my mission activities, and as I look down, while flying overhead, on the Togoba Leper Colony, which was my first mission appointment, I gain a new satisfaction. Most of the early buildings have been rebuilt. The addition of specialists on the staff has greatly improved the medical service. Spiritual emphasis is maintained in the institution. And my daughter Sharyn, only three years old when we carried her into Togoba on the day we took up our appointment, is now a trained nurse and a missionary to the needy lepers of New Guinea.

While trudging over the mountains of the interior, many a time I dreamed of the day when I would link up with a fellow missionary from the coast. Plans were even formulated mòre than once for such a rendezvous. Someday the jungle would part and hands be clasped as a highland missionary joined hands with one from the lowland. Likewise, for over half a century, while battling the treacherous seas of steamy Papua, many an Adventist missionary has wistfully scanned the distant blue of the soaring highlands and dreamed of the day when its slopes would be conquered for Christ.

Now we have mission aircraft, the method of bringing to pass these visions of future achievements.

My carefully laid plans for advance were only interrupted by the accident. For over two years I had been working toward the day when I would strike deeply into the upper reaches of the mighty Fly River and then fan outward. The initial target was Kiunga, six hundred miles up the river and only a few miles from the West Irian border. While it would take the mission vessel eight long days plugging upstream from the mouth of the meandering, sluggish Fly River to reach Kiunga, I could fly there from Laiagam in seventy-five minutes.

Finally, a day was set for this advance move—April 17, 1968. Tools, supplies, and evangelistic aids were gathered. Pastor Paul Piari, the proven pioneer, was selected to lead. Two other highland missionaries, Timothy and Sambai, were chosen to assist Paul. Several days prior to this move were spent in special Bible study and prayer.

For two days before our departure storm clouds continually chased each other over the ridges. Since I had not seen Kiunga before, and since it was surrounded by vast swampy flats devoid of landmarks, I needed reasonable weather to locate it. But the morning of my departure dawned bright and clear. My wife was relieved, and I was delighted. Smoothly mounting the early morning sky, I set course, treetop clouds covering the jungle of the plains. After seventy-five minutes of flying, my passengers and I saw Kiunga obligingly appear over the aircraft's nose through a small hole in the clouds.

As soon as we landed, our missionaries tumbled excitedly out of the aircraft and unloaded the tools and supplies. A visit to the local government officers found them cooperative, and a quick survey of the locale found the New Guineans friendly. Two other Christian mission organizations had preceded us to the area. They were neighborly, and there was plenty of work for all here.

When I returned five days later, Paul joyfully informed me that a village six miles deep in the jungle had welcomed him. I flew over it and saw that posts had already been erected in a clearing for his house and a start made on a garden. Crowds flocked to hear the message of hope. This clan had only recently moved into the area from a remote part of the jungle, and the gospel deeply appealed to their parched hearts.

Several weeks later I flew to Daru on the coast to contact our missionaries there. Pastor John Richardson, president of the Papuan Gulf Mission, and veteran Pastor Sydney Stocken greeted me. From there we went up the river by boat to the Oriomo River mission station, Pastor Stocken's headquarters. After spending a delightful Sabbath day there, we traveled four hours downstream at night with the aid of a spotlight.

As the morning mists were dissipating, we three boarded the aircraft with Papuan evangelist Maino, who spoke the Papuan language and who was to assist Pastor Paul for a few weeks.

After landing at Kiunga, we shook hands as a symbol of the linking of our highland mission endeavour with that of the lowlands. Thus the dreams of many intrepid missionaries came true. And this without aching bones or bruised limbs from weeks of trudging over mountains or along swampy lowland trails—all made possible by our mission aviation program. In one swift move we had burst the bounds of the mountain barriers and had plunged deeply into the heart of Papua.

A few weeks later, on one of my regular visits, I arrived over

Kiunga only to find that the clouds at treetop level offered no openings to locate the airstrip and land. The radio reported that the nearest airstrip not weather-bound was Nomad River. This is the center of the fierce and dreaded Biamie tribe, the last known bastion of practicing cannibalism. Each clan of the Biamie people lives in constant fear of its neighbors. In front of each of their long houses these people have a fighting platform from which they shoot human-bone-tipped arrows smeared with poison. If an enemy reaches a hut, a heavy log crashes down on him as he stoops to pass through the low door.

Circumstances forced me to make this unscheduled visit to these neglected people. When I landed, since few planes visit this outpost, the Papuan policemen gathered. Then the Australian patrol officer walked down. While we were talking, a few furtive Biamie men gathered on the fringes, and finally we coaxed several of them to come to the aircraft. Grimy and sullen, they were armed with bows and arrows. Ludicrous bunches of grass hung from their waists at the back, while strips of bark cloth draped from their waists in the front. Obviously these people fear all strangers just as they are feared by their neighbors, and the difficult clans were resisting all attempts by the government to pacify them. This timely contact with the government officer showed us that he was most helpful and anxious that we join in efforts to civilize the area.

A short time later I was pleased to take missionary Milton Hook and two of his national assistants from his mission headquarters into Nomad, where a hut was built beside the airstrip. These depraved people present a terrific challenge, but from this humble newly established base messengers of the gospel will offer love for hatred and peace for hostility.

On the northwestern coast of Australian New Guinea is the Sepik District—also part of my flying domain. The vast Sepik plains are similar to the Papuan lowlands. At Ambunti, 450 miles up the Sepik River and approximately the center of the area, is missionary David Lundstrom, whose expansive parish includes the May River whose banks are made gloomy with continual stories of intertribal killings.

Having returned from a nine-day patrol by boat and foot to this area in July, 1968, David requested me to drop urgently needed supplies to two of his outposts. Seven people had just been murdered, and he had recently established a new station in the midst of these dangerous people. To keep in contact with his national workers he had selected an airstrip site, which we were to inspect from the air this day.

For two ear-splitting hours we flew with the aircraft door removed, dropping tools, food, mail, and school supplies. At one village the villagers with the national evangelist and his wife waved exultantly below. Two weeks previously the woman had lost her baby at birth because there was no medical aid or transport.

A few weeks after our entry into the Kiunga area there was an amazing occurrance. A girl eight years of age had become critically ill where our national workers were building the new mission station. The girl was comatose and about to die. The whole village gathered around and began to lament in typical heathen despair. When our leader saw the cause, he was touched by their hopelessness and was constrained to seek God earnestly for His intervention on their behalf.

Bidding the tumult to be quiet, he commanded them to bow their heads while he supplicated their compassionate heavenly Father, about whom they had only recently heard. After his simple prayer of faith, to the amazement of all the girl sat up and requested something to eat. The whole village was deeply moved and determined to follow their newly found Saviour, who had stooped to help them in their dire need.

Sometimes I am asked whether I believe the stories of these astonishing healings. To disbelieve them when whole villages attest to their verity would be perplexing. Then to ignore the evidence of one's eyes and also the deep joy of the parents or relatives of the restored ones would be bewildering. Who am I to limit the power of the omnipotent God who inhabits eternity, who has spread out the vast universe, and whose wisdom is revealed in the immensity of the revolving nebulae as well as in the whirling atoms?

Whether or not a person is raised from a deep coma or death itself matters not to me. He who created all things animate and inanimate—who redeemed me and all who believe—is able to do all these and greater miracles.

Many times I have been rebuked by the childlike faith of these humble people of the jungle whose minds are uncluttered by the "whys" and "hows" of our more sophisticated society. Perhaps James was troubled by similar thoughts when he wrote, "Hath not God chosen the poor of this world rich in faith, and heirs of the kingdom which He hath promised to them that love him?" James 2:5.

With divine foresight our Lord looked down to our godless age and was inspired to propose the provocative question, "Nevertheless when the Son of man cometh, shall He find faith on the earth?" Luke 18:8. Indeed He will, among the faithful of every land—including Papua and New Guinea.

While we pause to thank God for the modern marvels of this technological age which dramatically help us carry the gospel to "the uttermost part of the earth," it is still true that the *greatest* want of the world is the want of men—not radios or planes. Only as these inventions are sublimated to the urgent task of soul winning are they serving their Heaven-appointed purpose. The following words of a well-known poem could well echo the plaintive lament of New Guinea:

> *Bring me men to match my mountains,*
> *Bring me men to match my plains,*
> *Men with empires in their purpose*
> *And new eras in their brains. . . .*
> *Men whose thoughts shall prove a highway*
> *Up to ampler destinies,*
> *Pioneers to clear thought's marshlands*
> *And to cleanse old error's fen;*
> *Bring me men to match my mountains—*
> *Bring me men!*
> *—Sam Walter Foss.*

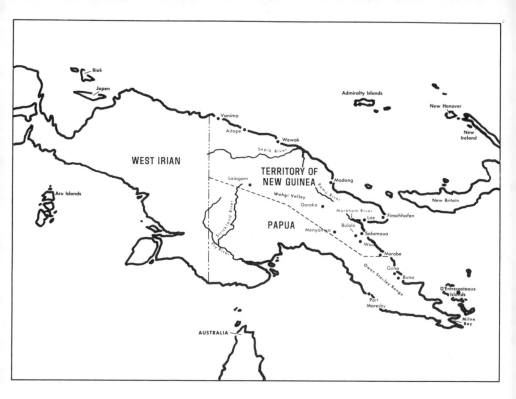

Towering, jungle-snarled mountains are the major physical features of the island of New Guinea.

When Len Barnard went to Papua New Guinea, the hills and valleys were filled with people who had no contact with the outside world.

Until after World War II, the islands of the South Seas were populated with tribes of people whose way of life centered around traditions and ceremonies passed on from generation to generation.

Deep in the folds of the interior highlands are people who are little more than a generation removed from cannibalism. Bedecked with feathers, paint, beetles, and shells, chiefs are ready for a Sing-Sing.

As a young couple who had grown up in New Zealand, Mavis and Len Barnard started their mission service in the Highlands of Papua New Guinea in 1948. For 26 years, they braved the dangers involved in pioneering with the Gospel among people who found it difficult to accept the white man.

As a young man, Paul Piari was notorious for his fighting prowess. When Christianity came to his valley, he was curious — and amazed to hear things from the 'black book.'

Piari, the fighter, became Paul, the preacher. With three assistants, he now pastors 18 churches and 10 companies scattered for 60 miles across the Western Highlands.

Piari reads and understands his English King James Bible, but he cannot speak the English language. As he preaches, he translates the message to Pidgin or into his native tongue of Enga.

Barnard placed his hand on Piari's shoulder and asked how many people he had baptized. Piari replied, "Plenty more!"
"This man," says Barnard, "has walked where no other mortal has dared to go."

Photo: Leonard Barnard
Len Barnard and Paul Piari attended the 1966 General Conference session
held in Detroit, Michigan. With artifacts and Pidgin English, they captured the
attention at Service Clubs around the city where they were invited to speak.

When Barnard started the leprosarium at Togaba, Kai was a young leper who came for treatment and always attended worship. He was one of the first group to be baptized by Len. He is holding a Kur stone which symbolizes the evil spirit he worshiped before he became a Christian.

For 36 years, Kai has been using his Picture Roll to tell about the love of God. He does not know how many people have been won to the Lord, but those who know him best say there are hundreds.

Kai says, "Leg belong me no good. Hand belong me no good. Skin belong me no good. Neck belong me good fella." He means that his hands and feet and skin are not in good condition, but his voice is strong. He can tell others about the God who cares for him.

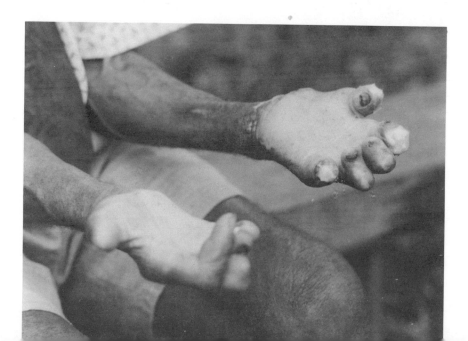

In 1964, after having solicited the funds himself, Len Barnard purchased the first Adventist mission plane in the South Pacific. Villages that had taken days to reach by foot became accessible in minutes.

Photo: Leonard Barnard

As the Gospel has spread across Papua New Guinea, many young nationals have become pastors. Using tattered Picture Rolls, they go out and teach children about Jesus.

Today the people of Papua New Guinea have changed their way of life. Their faces glow with happiness. Two times each day, pastors and lay leaders meet with the people to study the Sabbath School lesson in a language they can understand. More than 700 languages and dialects are spoken in Papua New Guinea — Pidgin English is the catalyst.

In a most remarkable way, Christianity has gained acceptance in the cloistered mountain world of Papua New Guinea. Seventh-day Adventist missions have been a strong force in bringing changes to the people.

In 1988, Len Barnard visited the Western Highlands. In village after village, crowds gathered to welcome him home. Always before leaving, he prayed for "his people."

Hundreds awaited Len on the mountaintop at Porgera — such a remote village in the Western Highlands that it might well be termed "an uttermost part of the earth." As he looked out across the people, and as they displayed their love and affection, he experienced the only reward he had ever sought — people worshiping the God he had come to tell them about.

Sitting at the controls of a plane, Barnard reminisced. "I used to skirt those 12,000-foot ridges and lower the plane on to the village airstrips. I could cover in 15 minutes a distance that it used to take three days to walk."

On a tarmac at the Mt. Hagen airstrip, Len told Jerry Heinrich, author and producer of the HALL OF FAITH series, how his accident happened that nearly cost his life.

The accident will ever be a reminder of God's healing power and the answer to the prayers of thousands who turned to God and in Pidgin English pleaded for Len's recovery.

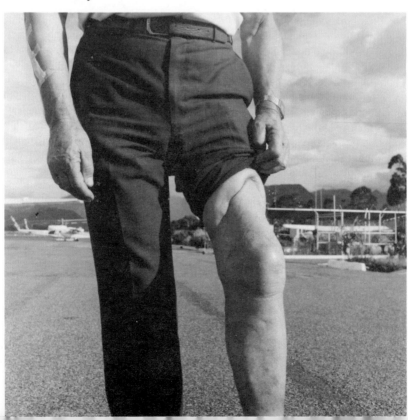

With 7,000 air hours, Barnard organized the Adventist Aviation Association with base headquarters at Avondale College. The purpose of the organization is to involve laymen to go out and teach people in outback villages and throughout the remote areas of the South Pacific.

Barnard's "Andrew Stewart" is mounted beside Ellen White's home at Avondale College in Australia.

Len Barnard, A MEMBER OF THE MISSION SPOTLIGHT HALL OF FAITH, pioneered the Third Angel's Message in Papua New Guinea. He walked steep mountain trails, paddled the crocodile-patroled rivers, made his way across snake-infested swamplands, and braved the dangers of the natives themselves.